lead the way
GOD
made
you

Larry Shallenberger

Loveland, Colorado

Visit our Web site: **www.group.com**

Credits
Editor: Mikal Keefer
Chief Creative Officer: Joani Schultz
Copy Editor: Elaine Davis
Art Director/Print Production Artist: Pamela Poll
Cover Art Director/Designer: Bambi Eitel
Cover Photographer: Rodney Stewart
Interior Illustrator: Steve Bjorkman
Production Manager: Peggy Naylor

Library of Congress Cataloging-in-Publication Data
Shallenberger, Larry, 1968-
  Lead the way God made you : discovering your leadership style in children's ministry / by Larry Shallenberger.-- 1st American pbk. ed.
       p. cm.
  ISBN 0-7644-2823-3 (pbk. : alk. paper)
  1. Church work with children. 2. Christian leadership. I. Title.
  BV639.C4S52 2005
  259'.22--dc22
                              2005001492

Printed in the United States of America.
10 9 8 7 6 5 4 3 2 1   14 13 12 11 10 09 08 07 06 05

dedication

To my parents who taught me to love and serve the church from a young age.

To Amy: My best friend and lover. Thanks for your support. Anyone who gets a thing out of this book owes you a debt of gratitude. Thanks for cheerfully allowing me to log the hours on this book.

To Alex, Nathaniel, and Cole: I love you all. I can't wait to discover together the way that God has wired you to lead.

And to my wonderful volunteer team. Thank you all for allowing me to grow, develop, fail, and reinvent myself as a leader. I wouldn't trade my team for any team out there.

Special thanks to the those who have stayed with me since the beginning—Bill, Craig, Peg, Kim W., Kim G., Doree, and Irene. Especially Irene for being such a different leader than I am—thanks for showing me how to think more like a Stage Manager.

Years ago, Chris Yount asked me to try my hand at writing a magazine article. You changed my life, Chris. Thanks.

Mikal Keefer: Only a 6-foot-7-inch man like yourself could hold so much humor, integrity, and talent. Thanks for being a giant in these areas. Thanks for your friendship and tutoring. I'm a better person and writer for knowing you.

Thom and Joani Schultz: You've built a constellation of ideas that points us all to Jesus. I keep bumping into Jesus during my trips to Loveland. Thanks for teaching me how to serve him better.

Derek: Each year that I've known you, you have become an increasingly more effective leader, husband, father, and friend. Thanks for being an example to me.

table of **contents**

introduction

I have a confession to make: My name is Larry and I once suffered from a serious case of Leadership Style Envy.

LSE isn't pretty, and I can remember precisely where I was sitting when I knew that my condition needed immediate attention.

During my college years, when I was preparing for ministry, I attended Willow Creek Community Church.

One night Bill Hybels laid out his vision for the church. I sat helplessly in the balcony as Hybels pressed every button on my internal dashboard. My drive for the church was reborn. Truth be told, I entered that room tired and jaded from years of theology course work.

I left the building renewed in my enthusiasm for serving the church. But I also found myself thinking about how Hybels had cast the vision with so much power and energy. Try as I might, I couldn't picture myself standing where he'd stood, connecting like he had connected, the vision pouring out and hanging in the air so real you could almost touch it.

I found myself thinking: "Why can't *I* lead like that? What's wrong with *me*?" God used Hybels to plant seeds of hope in me, while darker motives planted seeds of jealousy.

Fast-forward the tape about seven years. I'd graduated and was leaving a job in children's mental health to become a children's pastor. Part of what attracted me to join the staff of my church was the chance to work with a friend of mine.

Derek Sanford is an amazing visionary leader. Parachute Derek into any crowd on the planet and within 10 minutes Derek will organize the mob, motivate them with a dream, and launch them to take the world for God. When I came on staff, I watched his style and his success and began comparing myself to him.

Derek was every inch the classic, Hybels-esque leader I wished I could be. Yet I was…well, the truth was I didn't know *what* type of leader I was. Being a children's pastor required a different range of leadership skills than I'd used as a children's mental health case manager. That much was clear.

But if I wasn't a visionary leader, then what was I?

I was leading…and I'll bet you are, too.

People were following me…and they're following you, too.

But I wasn't Bill Hybels or Derek Sanford…and maybe you aren't, either.

I should have focused on discovering *my* style, and *my* leadership voice. Instead, I wasted time wishing I could be a vision-casting visionary leader like Derek. I settled for jealousy and leadership-envy instead of growing into who God was calling me to be.

And perhaps that's where you find yourself, too. Maybe you're also a charter member of the Grand Order of Leadership Style Envy. If so, welcome. You're not alone.

Most of the leadership books out there are all about teaching people to be visionary leaders. And there's a part of our roles as children's ministry leaders that calls for us to communicate vision for our ministries. But that doesn't mean we're all wired as visionary leaders.

This book is for every person called to children's ministry who is looking to find his or her own leadership voice. You might discover you're a visionary who can lead like a Craig Jutila, a Sue Miller, or a Jim Wideman. But then again, you might not.

The point is that you'll discover *your* leadership style by the end of this book. And you'll know how to leverage your style in your church context to accomplish God's will in your children's ministry.

The process starts with a self-test that will help you figure out how God has wired you. Then we'll dig into principles that will help you grow as an individual leader *and* help make your ministry team interdependent. This works whether you're in a church of 70 or 7,000.

As you learn about the leadership styles of the people on your children's ministry team, you'll understand how your styles complement each other, and how you can protect each other's weaknesses.

Once you've discovered your natural style, you'll learn how to broaden your leadership voice by learning skills from other styles. I'm still *not* a natural visionary leader, and there's little chance I'll ever become Bill Hybels.

Yet, I've learned how to do visionary stuff while still being true to—and benefiting from—my natural style of leadership. Instead of trying to be something I'm not, I'm able to work from the strengths God has given me.

> **Once you've discovered your natural style, you'll learn how to broaden your leadership voice by learning skills from other styles.**

I'm convinced of this truth: After you've discovered your natural leadership style and you're content with how God wired you, you're free to take on parts of other leadership styles and make them your own.

In his book *Primal Leadership*, Daniel Goleman makes the argument that a person can grow in *any* leadership skill if he or she is willing to attack the problem with unwavering discipline.[1] It's hard work to grow as a leader, and it's nearly impossible to do if you're carrying the personal baggage of jealousy and covetousness.

So that's my leadership confession: I once suffered from Leadership Style Envy. What's your confession? Are you unsure of who you are as a leader? Do you wonder if you're a leader at all? Are you wondering whether God chose the right person when he placed you in children's ministry leadership?

Perhaps you know who you are. You just can't figure out why the other people on your team are incapable of thinking like you do. Perhaps your team is filled with such diverse people that you aren't sure you'll ever all come together to get the job done. You privately wonder why God threw you into this impossible, interpersonal jumble.

My prayer is that by the time you are finished using this book—taking the test, working through the results, asking your team to do the same—you'll be confident in God's wisdom in placing you right where you are.

That's the heart of this story. You *are* a leader. God has *intentionally* placed you at your church, in your team, and with your kids. God's plans are true, wise, and at times, infuriating from our perspective.

Use this book as a map and a guide for your life journey of understanding why you are here for "such a time as this."

Shape the Future!

Larry Shallenberger

Endnote

1. Daniel Goleman, Richard Boyatzis, and Annie McKee, *Primal Leadership: Realizing the Power of Emotional Intelligence* (Harvard Business School Press, 2002). In my view, this is a "must read" for every serious ministry leader. Chapter Six deals specifically with a self-guided learning plan for improving your leadership skills.

there's **no such thing** as a **perfect leader** (and that includes you)

the myth of the perfect leader

Picture the perfect leader. Got that person in mind?

What does he or she look like? Does your perfect leader have the charisma of a Kennedy, good looks worthy of People magazine, and the genius of a Stephen Hawking?

The Myth of the Perfect Leader permeates our society. We *love* believing that somewhere out there is a man or woman who's able to defend us from our enemies, provide a chicken in every pot, make the sun shine a little brighter, and be a role model for our children.

We desperately want to believe in this do-all and end-all Perfect Leader, and that desire plays out in a variety of ways in our society…

- **In business,** we bankroll CEOs with gargantuan salaries and give them privileges and perks to match. Why? All in the hope that the Perfect Leadership will protect our jobs and investments, and lead us all to wealth.

- **In entertainment,** Marvel Comic heroes attract record crowds to the theaters.[1] We'll gladly pay a small fortune for a ticket and bag of popcorn so we can watch Perfect Leaders use their super powers to protect us from super villains.

- **In politics,** every four years, Americans look for a Perfect Leader to run the country. Americans want a president who can handle economic forces and foreign policy with equal, excellent skill. We want a president who'll inspire us, lead without compromise, tame Congress, love his or her spouse, and guide America into peace and prosperity.

If you don't live in America, don't point fingers: You probably want the same from *your* country's leader, too.

Most people are looking for a leader who can do all, be all, and solve all.

Unfortunately, churches also have bought into the myth of the Perfect Leader. We want a pastor who preaches like Billy Graham, counsels like Dr. Phil, budgets like Donald Trump, strategizes like General Patton, comforts like Mother Teresa, and inspires like Bill Clinton—and we want the leader to perform each of these functions with equal levels of brilliance.

Perhaps we long for a Perfect Leader because we feel the need for a strong warrior to tame our dangerous world. Or maybe it's because we want our Perfect Leader to give us a dream worth chasing.

Whatever the cause, here's the bottom line: Most people are looking for a leader who can do all, be all, and solve all. One person who'll be everything we need.

Friend, that sets you and me up for failure.

Why? Because when we're introduced as the "leader" of a children's ministry—even if our entire organization is ourselves and two volunteers—people compare us against the myth of the perfect leader.

Even worse: We compare *ourselves* against that myth.

Everyone who measures herself or himself against that perfect leader yardstick feels inadequate. Buy into the myth and you'll either

kill yourself by trying to live up to it, or you'll feel inadequate and underachieving.

Either choice is an ugly one, because both options force you to distort who God has called and equipped you to be. When we try to be someone God didn't wire us to be, we make it very hard for God to use us.

shattering the perfect leader myth

It's time to shatter the Myth of the Perfect Leader once and for all.

Here's how we'll topple that statue: by looking at what's required of leadership in a "five star" children's ministry.

"Five star" is a designation of excellence. Entertainment critics award a five-star rating to an excellent production—a play or movie that runs in the theater for months and that hits a level of excellence that's not often attained.

Nobody gives a play a five-star rating; the producers *earn* it. They earn it by making sure every piece of their production is outstanding and that every element works together. Down at the community playhouse nobody notices that the set design is spectacular if the acting is terrible.

You can always spot a five-star production at a theater. The reviews are respectful. Lines wrap around the building as sold-out shows are filled by enthusiastic patrons. It's hard to get a ticket because of the high demand. And the demand rolls on week after week, season after season.

In some way, an outstanding children's ministry is a lot like a five-star theater production.

Five-star children's ministries attract crowds of parents and children. These ministries are able to sustain momentum for years. They're designed to thrive over extended periods of time. And just as a winning theatre production has outstanding producers providing leadership, there's excellent leadership in a five-star children's ministry.

Let's look at each of the "five stars" a children's ministry needs to have in place if it's to become a blockbuster organization. These stars represent core leadership functions your ministry (and church) must have in place to be healthy and become outstanding.

Keep in mind that all *five* of these leadership elements must be in place for a ministry to be truly effective. Yet these five stars are *so* large and *so* all-encompassing that one leader can't possibly deliver them all.

Here are the five stars…

⭐ star one: describing a promised land

Every organization needs a "Promised Land," a preferred destination the group is moving toward. In most organizations *which* destination isn't important; what counts is that it's a place the organization (and the people in it) would prefer to be instead of staying where they are.

Consider Moses. He led the people of Israel from slavery toward a "land of milk and honey." That distant, unknown land was where people wanted to be, so much so that they packed up and headed off into an uncertain future so they could reach the dream.

We usually use the word *vision* instead of *Promised Land*, but the idea is the same: Moses described a place where slavery would be a thing of the past and where the people of Israel would be surrounded by rich resources. The people of Israel bought into Moses' vision, and it motivated them to take action.

The vision of a Promised Land energizes people in organizations. It motivates them to move toward an exciting future. When a leader focuses people on a vision, they'll chase dreams, achieve the impossible, and sometimes even change the world.

You can tell a Promised Land vision is important because of what happens when a group of people *doesn't* have a clear vision. Proverbs 29:18a says, "Where there is no vision, the people are unrestrained" (New American Standard Bible).

In your ministry, you need a Promised Land vision if you're going to have an excellent, five-star organization. But it *does* matter what that vision is. Without God's revealed vision, your ministry will be unfocused, undisciplined, and underachieving. Your people need a vision…but it must be *God's* vision for your ministry.

So here's the first challenge for the Perfect Leader: to discover God's Promised Land for his or her organization. Plus, the Perfect Leader must communicate that vision and convince the rest of the membership to "buy in."

And that's just the *beginning* of the Perfect Leader's responsibilities…

⭐ star two: providing road maps

It's not enough for an organization to know what its Promised Land looks like. The organization also needs to know how to *get* there. Unless God outfits your group with a pillar of fire and a cloud, you're going to need road maps to get to your goal.

There are two types of Organizational Road Maps.

• The first type is a strategic plan.

A strategic plan breaks down the journey to the Promised Land (fulfilling your ministry's vision) into a series of logical steps that need to be accomplished to move you from where you are to where you want to be.

Here's the first challenge for the Perfect Leader: to discover God's Promised Land for his or her organization.

Imagine that your "Promised Land" is starting an after-school program for unchurched children in your neighborhood. This vision is so compelling it keeps you up at night. You imagine dozens of families joining your church and coming into a friendship with Jesus—all because you met the needs of children. In your mind it's a beautiful picture, something that's all but accomplished.

But there are some practical questions that need to be answered. Who will volunteer to staff this project? How will you fund this program? Do you need approval from your church's governing board? If so, how will you get it? Where will you house this program? How will you advertise the program to your neighbors? An organized answer to these questions is essentially your strategic plan.

• The second kind of road map is a list of core values.
Core values describe *how* a ministry goes about its business. For example, a church with a core value of "creativity" probably emphasizes programs like drama and music in its worship service. A ministry that is living out a core value of "excellence" will be filled with staff and volunteers who execute their roles with precision.

Core values are to your church what DNA is to your body.

In each of your cells, there are spiral strands of chemicals that contain a code that determines how every cell in your body develops. As new cells are created, the DNA tells them what to do and where they fit. Having all your cells be on the same page is essential for your body to function.

Every church or ministry has a set of core values, whether the ministry knows it or not. Those core values reflect what's most important, what gets done when there's too little time to do everything. Core values reflect how people treat each other. A ministry's core values become a road map that determines the quality and culture of the organization.

And those core values can tell an observer if the ministry is likely to get to the Promised Land it has chosen.

examples of common core values

- **Servanthood**—"Around here we're all gifted by God to be servants."

- **Biblical truth**—"We embrace biblical truth and seek to live it daily."

- **Excellence**—"Second best isn't good enough."

- **Creativity**—"We worship a Creator and reflect his creative nature."

- **Team-based**—"Where two or more are gathered, good things happen."

- **Healthy relationships**—"We don't gossip, and we speak the truth in love."

For instance, if you have a vision of a thriving after-school program and your church doesn't value children, you're in trouble. No matter how powerfully you present your vision to the church board, your program proposal will be shot down. What you want to do is essentially at odds with what your church values.

That means a leader who is able to provide road maps has two choices when he or she has a clear view of where the church should be headed. The first option is to do the clear-headed planning that provides incremental steps that lead to fulfilling the vision.

The second option, assuming the core values of the church don't line up with where God is taking the ministry, is to help people grow into embracing the required core values—or at least challenging existing or fuzzy core values that present road blocks.

For instance, if your church is gung-ho about funding mission projects that help children in foreign lands but won't consider an after-school program to serve neighborhood kids, there's room for some discussion.

The strategic plan road map tells you how to logistically get to your Promised Land. The core value road map tells you what your ministry will be like when it gets there. Thriving churches pay attention to *both* maps.

Every ministry needs a leader who's responsible for creating these maps. If there's a Perfect Leader out there, this is his or her job.

star three: tending to the toolbox

In your ministry there are jobs that need to be accomplished. A *lot* of jobs.

Each individual job requires specific skills; knowledge; an awareness of policies, procedures, and values; and a deep understanding about how things get done in your children's ministry. Imagine that each of those skills, every piece of knowledge, and all that understanding were collected in a toolbox.

It would be a rather *large* toolbox, wouldn't it? Yet, everything in it is needed.

If a group of kids were running a corner lemonade stand, what would they need in their toolbox? They'd need to know how to mix lemonade, make change, set up a sturdy stand, acquire and use pitchers and glasses, choose a good location, and muster enough people skills to be friendly toward their customers.

Those are a lot of tools—and the kids are just peddling 50-cent glasses of lemonade!

Larger organizations—like your church or ministry—require *far* more tools. As a children's ministry worker, you're doing work that's often associated with a pastor, a counselor, and a program manager. Running the lemonade stand—your refreshment center—is the *simplest* part of your job.

Stocking your ministry's toolbox—making sure people have all the required skills—doesn't happen by accident. Someone needs to know what skills and knowledge are needed to pull off your children's ministry. Someone has to figure out who can provide those tools and recruit and train those people for children's ministry. As volunteers come and go, someone has to keep an eye on the toolbox to make sure necessary tools are present and in good repair.

> **What happens when a children's ministry doesn't have enough tools, or the right tools, to fulfill its vision and meet its goals?**

If you want your children's ministry to purr along without problems, someone's got to take the responsibility to know what tools are needed and to get them in the hands of the right people. Someone's got to train teachers and coach worship teams.

Someone's got to make sure that when a new program is launched, the right resources are available to make it successful, that the proper tools are in the toolbox.

That someone is a leader who's doing important, vital work!

What happens when a children's ministry doesn't have enough tools, or the right tools, to fulfill its vision and meet its goals? I'll tell you what happens—the same thing that happens to me when I pull my toolbox out of the car trunk and discover that I don't have the tool I need.

Recently my car's battery was near death, so I jumped it and scooted to a local auto supply store to replace the faltering battery. I was pleasantly surprised when the cashier asked if I wanted the store attendant to replace the battery for me.

"Why not?" I thought. I'm not particularly mechanical, and it was a cold, wet day.

I'll admit I felt a tinge of guilt as, from the comfort of my car, I watched an attendant struggle with the old battery. But the woman was a professional—how hard could it be?

Guilt turned to frustration when what should have been a five-minute job turned into a half hour, and the old battery was still sitting under the hood. Finally, I climbed out into the cold and asked what the problem was. Why was I still waiting?

I learned that the bolt holding the battery in place was stripped. The attendant had tried loosening the bolt every way possible, but it had become clear that only a bolt cutter with an unusually long handle was going to get the job done. Neither of us had one in our toolboxes, so I drove my car to my dad's house.

My father is a lift-truck mechanic. It took him about 30 seconds to size up the problem, and then he went to his van—which is a giant toolbox on wheels. He found the correct tool, and within minutes we had the battery replaced.

When a children's ministry doesn't have the correct tools, it won't execute programs well. Tasks take longer, are done awkwardly, and people involved find themselves frustrated.

Every ministry needs a leader who is able to keep the corporate toolbox stocked properly. Without this leader in place, the ministry's wheels will sooner or later fall off.

If there's a Perfect Leader somewhere, you can add this to that individual's job description, too.

⭐ star four: keeping the ministry "heart-healthy"

Every children's ministry needs a healthy heart. By *heart* I mean a sense of optimism and well-being, a positive outlook that the ministry will achieve its vision and reach its Promised Land.

That sort of positive outlook won't happen unless the interpersonal relationships within the organization are healthy. It's important that the ministry doesn't grow self-centered and that people in it aren't distracted by fighting.

Remember Moses' struggles with the heart of his people? When Moses returned to Egypt, he not only had to convince Pharaoh to let God's people go, he *also* had to convince the Israelites that God was capable of rescuing them. In Exodus 6:9, Moses shared God's message of deliverance with the people, "but they did not listen to Moses on account of their despondency and bondage" (NASB).

The Israelites had lost their corporate heart. They weren't capable of being delivered until they had witnessed the 10 plagues and regained a sense of confidence in God.

Even after they'd left Egypt, the Israelites' "heart problems" continued to give Moses fits. The books of Exodus, Numbers, and Deuteronomy are filled with stories of Moses trying to manage the rotten attitudes of people who were on their way to the Promised Land. Moses had to deal with a challenge to his leadership, grumbling, and a constant lack of gratitude toward God. Each of these heart problems was a challenge that threatened to keep the Israelites from making it to the Promised Land.

Every children's ministry needs a leader who is responsible for managing the heart of the volunteers and staff. Morale needs to be bolstered. Tired workers need to be encouraged. Gossip needs to be squelched, and new lines of communication need to be opened. Ministry workers need to be schooled in healthy conflict management.

If there's a Perfect Leader out there somewhere, caring for the heart of the ministry is part of his or her job description.

star five: providing muscle

Finally, every organization needs muscle.

Muscle is the ability to get things done. Identifying your Promised Land and knowing where it's located are both good things. Having the expertise and the health to get there are vital.

But there comes a time when every member of your children's

ministry needs to actually *do it.* The kindest thing you can say about a church that has no muscle is that it had good intentions…but that's all.

I know of a church that has a file cabinet brimming with good intentions. The church secretary has neatly filed away every strategy plan the church has created in the past two decades. Each plan sports a professional binding, a newly polished mission statement, new goals, and minutes of meetings that show congregational approval.

But how many of those goals were ever accomplished?

None. Once the plans were completed and printed, the secretary filed them away and they were never seen again.

Why did the church leadership go to all the trouble to draft goals and strategies if there was never any intention of managing those plans to completion? What was the point?

I think the church leadership *intended* to accomplish the goals. Truly. But because the church lacked a system to inspect the progress being made on the goals, nothing happened. Without accountability, the church's energy shifted from the big-picture vision and goals to those week-to-week routines and crises that clamored for attention.

> **Too many of us make it a habit to live week to week without ever setting long-range goals at all.**

There were plenty of good intentions but absolutely no muscle, so nothing ever got done.

Before we children's ministry workers get smug about all the follow-through follies we observe happening at the top, let's remember that the church in question at least *had* goals. Too many of us make it a habit to live week to week without ever setting long-range goals at all.

It doesn't matter if your pastor is unorganized and doesn't follow through on goals. You're responsible for what *you* can do, not what your pastor can't do.

Every children's ministry needs a leader who's a strength trainer, someone who's responsible for modeling focus, having an intense work ethic, and helping the team set ambitious goals and measurable, calendared objectives.

Like any good trainer, this leader will review the goals with team leaders and help all members of the team keep their commitments to do what they said they would do.

Unless your Perfect Leader is adding muscle to the mix, he or she is falling short.

Just so we're clear: A Perfect Leader would, by definition, do an excellent job in these five areas of leadership:

Describing a Promised Land—providing a vibrant vision about where the ministry can be and how it can look in the future;

Providing Road Maps—describing in detail the steps that will lead to seeing the vision actualized and to reaching the desired Promised Land;

Tending to the Toolbox—guaranteeing that all the skills and knowledge needed to do ministry are available and current at all times;

Keeping the Ministry "Heart-Healthy"—attending to interpersonal and morale issues and encouraging the troops to grow spiritually as they march forward into the future; and

Providing Muscle—leading the charge by organizing and executing all the tasks that must be accomplished to move your ministry forward.

Quite the job description.

one leader can't do it all

Think about the people God has placed in your ministry. In your church. In your *country*.

Is there really one person who can hang all five of the stars in your ministry constellation? No way—it's not possible. No one person can get all these jobs accomplished without destroying his or her health, marriage, and friendship with God. The job is too great.

There is no Perfect Leader who's going to be able to do it all in your children's ministry. Not someone else…not you. Nobody can do it alone.

Still not convinced? If you're a United States citizen, visit www.census.gov and look up how many children under the age of 14 live in your county. If you live in another country, check your government's census information Web site for the same information.

Now plug the appropriate number into the following statement and read it aloud: "The mission of my children's ministry is to help _____ children enter into a growing friendship with Jesus. I'll make that happen this year."

Still think there's a Perfect Leader out there somewhere who could live up to that mission statement? Who could fulfill all five of the leadership functions with excellence?

I didn't think so.

So here and now let's declare the Myth of the Perfect Leader dead and gone. It's time to admit *you're* not that Perfect Leader…*I'm* not that Perfect Leader…that Perfect Leader doesn't *exist*.

But that's not a problem—because your ministry can still have all five leadership stars represented and in place. There's a better way for that to happen.

how to have all five stars in your children's ministry

If we've just killed off the Perfect Leader, then who's going to be in charge?

Apparently mere mortals—like us.

It's time we return to the biblical concept of leadership responsibilities being shared by a team. I'm *not* saying that God doesn't appoint point people within every congregation to be the final authority for a ministry. But no point person can be expected to embody all five stars. In situations where the entire burden is placed on one person, it's inevitable that a falling-star sighting will follow.

Maybe you're the sole person on the staff at your church who focuses on children's ministry. Maybe you're paid; maybe you're a volunteer. Maybe you're full time or part time. Doesn't matter. What counts is this: If an alien spacecraft landed in your church parking lot and the little green men asked to be taken to the children's ministry leader, everyone would point at you.

You're it.

Like me, you may *not* be the visionary leader so many people expect you to be.

Well, listen and listen well: *That's not a problem.*

God's put you in your role, which means that how he wired you to lead others will work. It just won't work if you insist on trying to handle all the leadership functions yourself or if you pretend to be the Perfect Leader who can cover all the bases.

Imagine how dramatically you could improve your ministry—and your own attitude—if you led others from your strengths instead of feeling like a misfit. How secure would you feel if you didn't have to fret about whether your leadership style was OK?

Things would get better, trust me. They got better for me—and they will for you.

In the next chapter of this book you'll take the Dramatic Leadership Assessment Test. Don't worry about the name: I promise you *won't* be tested on your dramatic abilities. No singing or dancing is required.

The word *dramatic* refers to the process by which groups of people put on a play in the theatre. There are six distinct leadership functions required to pull together a successful play—and each function connects to one of the five stars I just finished describing.

You'll soon discover a great deal about your natural leadership style. You'll then explore how your style (or styles) complement other styles, and how you can work with team members to accomplish tremendous things.

So get ready to be amazed at what God has done, and is doing, in you.

to review...

Next you'll take the test and discover how your leadership style fits into the six dramatic leadership functions I'll explain later. Then you'll work through six chapters that describe each style in detail.

If you're like most people, you might be tempted to skip the rest of the book and just read up on your own style.

That would be a mistake.

If you must, read about your leadership style first. That's fine. But don't close the book there. By studying *all* the styles, you'll discover why the other leaders in your life don't think like you. Why they make decisions differently than you do. Why they're doing stuff that makes sense to them, but sometimes not to you.

Here's a leadership fact that's also a leadership weakness: We tend to surround ourselves with people who think like we do. It's easier and more comfortable. Nobody challenges us. That's the up side.

> **Here's a leadership fact that's also a leadership weakness: We tend to surround ourselves with people who think like we do.**

The *down* side is that you (and I) can't deliver five-star leadership all on our own. We *need* other leaders whose different styles of leadership complement our styles. Those leaders are the people best able to compensate for our weaknesses.

Plus, your children's ministry doesn't exist in a vacuum. Your church is filled with pastors, lay leaders, financial officers, and potential volunteers: Each one of them has the ability to influence your ministry in a positive or negative direction. By discovering the unique way that God made you and other leaders in your church, you'll begin to serve in the context of an authentic biblical community. You'll know where you fit best, and how to lead in ways that serve others.

That's how we live out our responsibility "to prepare God's people for works of service, so that the body of Christ may be built up until we all reach unity in the faith and in the knowledge of the Son of God and become mature, attaining to the whole measure of the fullness of Christ" (Ephesians 4:12-13).

Ready to start the adventure?

The test is just the turn of a page away. But before you move ahead, take time to consider the following questions. Answer them as honestly as you can.

for reflection and discussion

1. What type of leader is most respected within your ministry department or in your church? Why?

2. How can the belief that leadership looks a certain way hurt your ministry?

3. Look through the Five Stars. Which of the leadership functions seems most important to you? At first glance, who on your team seems strong in these five functions?

Endnote

1. At the time of this writing, *Spiderman* (2002) is already in fifth place for all-time top U.S. grossing films with $403,706,375 according to the International Movie Database (www.imdb.com).

CHAPTER ②

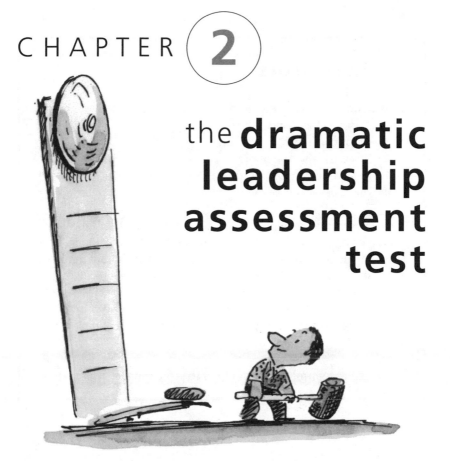

the **dramatic leadership assessment test**

Discover your leadership strengths with this powerful tool! You're about to discover your leadership strengths as you use this simple tool. But keep in mind that the assessment will reflect you clearly only if you describe who you really are, not the person you *wish* you were.

So answer honestly—and as quickly as you can.

Whatever you discover, it's who God made you...and it's good.

Whatever you discover, you've got strengths to bring to the leadership table. Strengths that God can use in you to build your children's ministry.

Whatever you discover—leadership is an adventure.

Ready?

Grab a pencil and get to it.

instructions

1. Respond to every statement on the Leadership Style Assessment Survey. Use the following scale:
   - **3**= This is constantly true of me
   - **2**= This is usually true of me
   - **1**= This is true of me sometimes; it's occasionally true
   - **0**= This is *never* true of me

2. As you respond, go with your first impulse. Don't think about what type of leader you wish you were. Don't compare yourself to other leaders. This inventory will help you identify your natural leadership style—but *only* if you don't try to "beat the test."

3. Write your response to the first statement in the #1 box in the Answer Grid. Write your response to the second statement in the #2 box in the grid, and so on.

You'll receive information about how to score the test after you've completed it.

leadership style assessment survey

1. I constantly find myself dreaming about the unrealized potential of my ministry.

2. I am able to mentally organize my ministry into a series of systems that need to be organized.

3. I am able to teach skills and concepts to my team members so they have the best chance for being successful in ministry.

4. I am primarily motivated by the belief that healthy ministries flow from healthy teams and individuals.

5. I am able to anticipate what supplies and labor the team will need to accomplish its goals.

Answer Grid

1	2	3	4	5	6
7	8	9	10	11	12
13	14	15	16	17	18
19	20	21	22	23	24
25	26	27	28	29	30
31	32	33	34	35	36
37	38	39	40	41	42
43	44	45	46	47	48

Place the total for each column below.

A	B	C	D	E	F

6. I quickly break large projects into a series of manageable steps.

7. I study both Scripture and other thriving ministries to discover in what direction I should lead my ministry.

8. I constantly look for new ways to improve the efficiency of how things happen in my ministry.

9. I can present both Scripture and my knowledge of children's ministry in simple and memorable ways that provoke people to change their behavior.

10. I constantly gauge the emotional and attitudinal health of my team.

11. I prefer to serve the people who are working with children than to work with kids myself.

12. I am able to quickly identify what resources, volunteers, and budgets need to be in place in order to lead my organization through change in an orderly fashion.

13. I feel satisfaction when I am able to mobilize my teams to tackle a big, formidable goal.

14. I take pleasure in creating an orderly environment in which people can serve.

15. I enjoy studying Scripture, as well as a broad field of literature in the business and education fields, in order to bring the best ideas into my ministry.

16. I feel most satisfied when there is a positive sense of well-being among my team members.

17. I enjoy working behind the scenes to support my more visible team members.

18. I enjoy it when my team leader turns to me to develop the plan to make his or her vision become a reality.

19. I enjoy being a pioneer and blazing a new path for my ministry.

20. I feel secure when I operate within clearly defined boundaries and expectations.

21. I feel most used by God when I am leading a classroom, whether it's filled with children or adults.

22. I enjoy tending to the personalities of my teams and ministry.

23. I take pride in my flexibility and willingness to do whatever it takes to get the job done.

24. I feel most valuable to the team when my skills are used to help the team move through change with efficiency and with minimal levels of conflict.

25. I lead by telling stories of what our ministry could look like.

26. I lead by creating policies and systems to help others do their jobs well.

27. I constantly create opportunities to equip my team members in group or individual settings.

28. I am able to lead my teams through powerful emotional experiences that shape my team members' attitudes and morale.

29. I tend to volunteer for the set up and tear down phases of most events.

30. I lead by developing calendars, timelines, and to-do lists that help our team measure its progress as we move toward our goals.

31. I have an easy time asking people to make deep personal sacrifices for the sake of the ministry achieving "the dream."

32. I have an eye for detail and am constantly generating to-do lists to organize my day.

33. I have identified a curriculum of skills and theory that I believe my team members need to understand in order to be effective children's ministers.

34. I am able to unite a diverse group of people into a common culture using training, symbols, experiences, and music.

35. I lead by doing all the menial jobs that can pile up and get in the way of the team accomplishing its goals.

36. I lead by helping the team and congregation manage their emotional responses to a large task or change by giving them constructive opportunities to share their opinions and feelings.

37. I often feel as if I am waiting for others in my ministry to catch up or get "on board."

38. I have difficulty understanding those who ignore details and protocol.

39. I am frustrated when my team members do not take advantage of the teacher training opportunities available to them.

40. I become frustrated when I see team members exhibiting attitudes that harm our group's well-being.

41. I can find myself feeling forgotten by the rest of the team.

42. I am frustrated by leaders who initiate change before taking the time to think through all of the implications of that change.

43. I am annoyed by people who have a hard time seeing the big picture.

44. I dislike working in unstructured environments.

45. I often find myself analyzing teachers whom I sit under and find myself developing better ways to present the same material.

46. I am frustrated by leaders who act without considering how their behavior will affect the team's morale.

47. I can be judgmental of team members who overlook the physical jobs that need to be done in the ministry.

48. I am frustrated by leaders who deviate from a plan on which the team has agreed.

Once you've filled in the answer grid, total up your scores in each column. You'll have a total for each of the letters A, B, C, D, E, and F.

Place your totals for each letter in the appropriate box on the key. The higher the number, the more prominent the Dramatic Leadership Style. You probably have a score for each of the six Dramatic Leadership Styles; that's typical.

Circle the letters of the two highest scores and the two lowest scores. Pay special attention to the chapters that deal with those Dramatic Leadership Styles as you read the remainder of this book.

KEY

Letter	My Point Total	Dramatic Leadership Style
A		**Director:** In theater, the director has the ability to "see" the production in its final form. The director uses that picture to motivate his or her team to action. In a ministry context, the Director provides vision for the ministry.
B		**Stage Manager:** In theater, the stage manager leads by administrating the countless details to be accounted for if the production is to be a success. In a ministry context, the Stage Manager provides ministry with efficiency.
C		**Drama Coach:** In theater, the Drama Coach leads by equipping the actors with all of the skills needed to give a convincing performance. In a ministry context, the Drama Coach instills the needed skills, methods, and philosophies to frontline team members.
D		**Theater Manager:** In theater, the Theater Manager provides the cast and crew with a warm, clean, and inviting environment. In a ministry context, the Theater Manager leads by making sure that the team is operating in a healthy emotional environment that fosters healthy ministry.
E		**Stagehand:** In theater, the Stagehand leads by meeting the physical needs of the team such as painting the sets or managing the props. In a ministry context, the Stagehand leads by tending to the physical needs of ministry so other team members can focus on their roles.
F		**Production Assistant:** In theater, the Production Assistant breaks down all the tasks that must be accomplished so the Director's vision can be realized on opening night. In a ministry context, the Production Assistant translates the Director's vision into logical and measurable tasks. This allows the whole team to manage change harmoniously.

CHAPTER (3)

the **director**

Debbie leaned forward in her chair, *transfixed by the show unfolding on the stage. She wasn't holding a $75 ticket to a Broadway show. There were no big names, big orchestra, or big lights. Nothing was big about this show. In fact, the average size of the actors was about three feet, four inches.*

Debbie was attending her niece's school musical, and her mind was exploding with possibilities. What if the children's ministry at her church staged a musical?

Debbie scanned the full auditorium, taking a quick inventory of all the relatives who'd come to see their loved ones on stage.

"If we held a musical at church, think of how many unchurched family members of our children would come out to see them! This would be a fantastic outreach event," she thought.

Debbie observed how disciplined every child was on stage.

Children knew their parts, knew where to stand, knew where to look. Collectively, the children were working as a team.

Debbie's mind whirled.

"Imagine the discipleship opportunities a musical would provide for our children! Our kids would have a chance to serve the church in a meaningful way. The kids would learn some valuable skills. They'd grow in confidence. Think about how close they'd grow!"

Debbie couldn't sleep that night. She lay awake dreaming about a kid's musical at her church.

Debbie was on the phone to her senior pastor as soon as it was a polite hour to call. She poured out her vision for the musical but didn't get the immediate green light she'd wanted.

Instead, Pastor Jack offered a carefully measured dose of supportiveness. He advised her to do more research, then bounce the idea off the other Sunday school teachers.

Debbie was disappointed in Pastor Jack's tepid response but didn't give up. She scoured the shelves of the local Christian bookstore, pulling out every children's musical. Two hours later she was triumphant: She left the store with a videotape of the perfect musical tucked under her arm.

Debbie then called every Sunday school teacher in her church. Her enthusiastic pitch was met with mixed responses. Patricia interrupted with questions. "Would we need elder approval for this? Is there a budget?" Tom and Susie were more open to the idea but didn't make any commitments.

So Debbie invited all the teachers and Pastor Jack over to her house to view the video together. Pastor Jack declined due to other commitments, but the rest of the group arrived promptly at 7 p.m. Debbie served hot popcorn and when the video wrapped up, she painted a vivid picture of how producing a musical would pump energy into the children's ministry.

The room was silent when Debbie finished.

"Well?" she demanded.

Tom spoke first. "I'm in. This is going to bring people together. It's going to be a great experience for the children and the church."

Susie threw her support in next, followed by Steve.

All eyes turned to Patricia, who wore a furrowed brow. Aware of the scrutiny she was receiving, she said, "I'm in too. I'm just thinking. A lot goes into producing a musical. It's not a matter of showing up and singing. This is a great idea. I'm just preoccupied by the details."

Debbie quickly cut in. She wasn't about to let her dream become derailed by a few details. "We'll deal with the details when the time comes. Right now I need to know who's in. Who wants to help bring the first kids' musical to First Church?"

All hands shot up quickly. Debbie took a mental note that Patricia raised her hand a full beat slower than everyone else did.

"All that needs to be decided is who is leading this team."

"It's your vision, Debbie. You're obviously the leader," Steve said. "I'm happy to help in any way I can. But you're the Director."

__The Director__. Debbie paused as the weight of the title settled on her shoulders.

profile of the director leadership style

On the Dramatic Leadership Assessment Test, you were identified as having a Director style of leadership. Good for you. We need Directors in children's ministry. But let's make sure—read this profile looking for traces of *yourself.*

If you took the test and you're sure a Director style *isn't* you, still scan this profile. You're probably rubbing shoulders with a Director somewhere in life, and this information will help you work most effectively with that sort of person.

A Director has an aptitude for seeing a God-shaped picture of what a children's ministry can look like in the future—a future characterized by the ministry living up to its full potential.

In theater terms, the Director can look into the future and see "Opening Night." If anybody is going to be casting a vision of how the final production will dazzle the audience, it's the Director.

learning the parts If you think you might be a Director, reread the "Profile of a Director" again, this time with a highlighter pen in hand. The profile is a composite description of Directors in general, but you know yourself best.

Customize the profile to fit yourself. Highlight sentences that your spouse or friends would point to and say, "Oh, yeah—that's you *exactly!*" Place a star next to sentences that don't describe you at all.

If you know you *aren't* a Director, decide if you have a Director in your life. Does this description remind you of anyone in your church or children's ministry? Jot down the names of those people below.

_____

_____

_____

_____

_____

In a children's ministry setting, the Director is able to visualize children's ministry on the stage of redemptive history. The Director sees children and volunteers in his or her church as actors boldly playing their parts, drawing a community into a vibrant friendship with Jesus.

In our opening story, Debbie looked into the future and saw a literal drama, one in which children were given the power to become missionaries to their peers in the context of a musical. We'll drop in on Debbie throughout this book to see how she's doing at getting the musical up and running. It becomes quite a learning adventure for her—and her church.

Debbie's Opening Night vision was a literal theater production, but the vision can take a variety of shapes.

For Nancy maybe it's an after-school program that tutors latch-key children. For Bob, Opening Night is a children's ministry that harnesses the power of the arts and media to communicate the message of the gospel in a way that makes sense to today's kids.

For you, maybe the vision is transforming your ministry from a teaching model to a discipleship model. You aren't content with children just knowing Bible stories; you want children to see themselves as growing followers of Jesus.

The number of Opening Night visions is as infinite as the God who plants them in the minds of Directors. If you've got a vision you're passionate about, that might be a good indicator that you've got some Director blood pulsing through your veins.

A person endowed with the Director leadership style is able to communicate Opening Night to his or her entire team with an intense passion. Like Debbie, who doggedly kept communicating her vision, a Director uses a variety of methods to tell the story of Opening Night. The Director keeps at it until he or she develops an energized core of people willing to follow the Director to make the Opening Night vision a reality.

A person with the Director leadership style constantly dreams about the unrealized potential of his or her children's ministry. Directors are change addicts who often find themselves blazing trails to new frontiers and pioneering new trails.

Another way to spot a Director is to see what bores the person.

Give a Director a task that requires lots of repetition and routine in the morning, and you can expect a resignation by 4:30 p.m. The status quo has no power to satisfy a Director—not with the next unclimbed mountain clearly in view.

When the Promised Land is on the horizon, Directors won't allow their teams to make camp in the fields of today. A Director is an agitated and shiftless soul, incapable of being pleased with yesterday's laurels.

Directors know that every trophy has an expiration date, and, like manna, those trophies aren't worth much the next day.

Directors also tend to study both Scripture and other growing children's ministries in a quest to gain a better view of what children's

> **A person with the Director leadership style constantly dreams about the unrealized potential of his or her children's ministry.**

ministry can become. They read, listen to tapes, and scrape together enough money to take classes and attend conventions.

Nothing feels more satisfying to Directors than realizing they have mobilized a diverse group of already busy people to tackle a big, formidable goal. Directors are willing to ask team members to make deep sacrifices so the team can achieve a spectacular Opening Night. Directors never seem to feel any embarrassment by the immensity of the requests they often make. They ask for the impossible because, well, that's what it's going to take to make the vision a reality.

Directors also have a strong sense of urgency. So strong, in fact, that they sometimes feel as if they're waiting for others in their ministries to catch up, to get "on board" with the dream. Directors chafe in the presence of people who don't share their sense of urgency.

If it sounds like a Director is a bulldozer, pushing through the vision no matter what, that's only *partially* true. Directors can easily be stopped dead in their tracks. All it takes is for people around the Director to be unwilling to buy into the Director's vision of Opening Night. At that point the Director is stymied, for all the Director's power lies in his or her ability to sell that vision.

> **Nothing feels more satisfying to Directors than realizing they have mobilized a diverse group of already busy people to tackle a big, formidable goal.**

Mature, God-honoring Directors serve the church well. Directors are the stewards of Promised Land visions. Through Directors' relentless drive to discover and communicate God's will, they provide direction for the whole church.

If your children's ministry is blessed with a Director—you, or someone else—you've got someone who has a gift of focus and a dream that will drive your ministry forward.

Directors also bolster the Healthy Heart star. Nothing builds a ministry's morale better than a clear, God-honoring purpose. Teams draw courage from their Director's confident reminder of the Promised Land that's out in the future. Desire and determination swell in the ranks as the team pushes ahead to achieve the impossible.

And the Muscle star is fortified as each member redoubles his or her efforts to cross the line into the Promised Land.

Bible case study: MOSES

In Chapter 1, I mentioned Moses and his vision of the Promised Land. Let's back up a moment and consider how Moses came to have this vision in the first place.

I believe God started brewing Moses' vision of God's people as liberated long before the famous burning bush experience.

Exodus, Chapters 1 and 2, tell us that Moses was born during evil times for the Israelites, who had migrated to Egypt during the great famine where they found both food and favor with the Pharaoh (Genesis 46).

Born the son of two Israeli slaves, Moses was raised by the Pharaoh's daughter as Egyptian nobility. He was educated as an Egyptian and was described as a being "powerful in speech and action" (Acts 7:22).

How old was Moses when he first recognized his true ancestry and when it occurred to him that freeing his people was possible? No one is absolutely certain, but this much is known: At some point, as Moses saw his kinsmen suffer under Egyptian task masters, Moses began to view himself a son of Israel rather than a son of Egypt (Hebrews 11:24, 25).

This identification with the slaves was so strong that when Moses saw a slave being beaten, he defended the slave. Moses struck down the Egyptian (Acts 7:24). Moses acted as a liberator.

If Moses expected his people to embrace him as an unexpected ally and rally around him, he was sorely disappointed. The slaves saw Moses as a lightning rod for Pharaoh's wrath and pulled away from him (Acts 7:25).

Not only was Moses not the liberator of his people, he was on his own.

So Moses ran away.

Moses ended up in Midian, where whatever vision he'd held for his people in Egypt apparently withered. Moses the Grand Liberator spent the next 40 years being a husband, raising two children, and working as a shepherd (Acts 7:29, 30).

Moses was 80 years old when God got his attention by speaking from a burning bush. God rekindled Moses' vision that God's people should be treated fairly rather than abused as slaves, but God added something: the Promised Land, a land flowing with milk and honey (Exodus 3:8).

Moses challenged God's wisdom in selecting him as a spokesperson. My hunch is that Moses was recalling his last, failed attempt to present himself as a liberator. Moses was convinced he wasn't credible, and small wonder: He'd already failed once to sell a vision of liberation to his people.

I believe that Moses' confidence in his ability to communicate a vision of freedom had been shattered by his past failure. Moses saw himself as inadequate for the task.

It was not an opinion God shared, and God provided Moses with a helper and signs to help Moses communicate.

So Moses set out for Egypt. A more reluctant visionary and fearful Director you'd be hard pressed to find.

for discussion and reflection

1. Have you ever felt inadequate to communicate a Promised Land to your team or congregation? What principles can you glean from Moses' story?

2. In what ways have you attempted to gain credibility when you feared that an audience or group of people wouldn't find you or your vision trustworthy?

contemporary case study: thirty minutes with brother jim

Children's Ministry Magazine recognized Jim Wideman as one of the pioneers in children's ministry over the past decade, and he's a senior voice in children's ministry. Brother Jim currently serves as the Director of Christian Education at The Church on the Move, the tenth largest church in America.

And Jim Wideman is a Director, through and through.

I called Jim and picked his brain about visionary leadership. Jim blew me away as he explained this type of leadership voice in such a down to earth manner…

LARRY: *Where do visions come from?*

JIM: My senior pastor just said in a sermon, "I don't have a great vision. A great vision has me." I love that.

You know, when I started out, I didn't know any other children's pastors. I didn't have a budget to pay for a workshop. I was forced to get my vision by going to God and saying, "What in the world do you want me to do?" If you'll do that, God will show you something that isn't happening in other churches.

LARRY: *Can you give me an example of a vision that has you?*

JIM: When I started out, some things frustrated me at the church where I served. Why was the Annual Meeting the least populated event on the church calendar? Why was it that when we elected deacons, we held a popularity contest instead of electing the people who were already "deking"?

Then I realized the answer to my own questions: No one trained these people as children to do these jobs!

Look at Samuel: Everything Samuel did for God as an adult, he learned as a kid. As a child he learned how to hear a tough message from God and deliver it to the right person. That's all Samuel did with his adult life, and he learned it as a child.

So my vision was to find out how adults serve in the church and to give kids hands-on training when they are young to do those jobs. We have children serving as ushers, greeters—you name it.

LARRY: *What would you tell a novice children's ministry leader, just setting out to develop his or her visionary leadership skills?*

JIM: Great visions come from finding a need and meeting it, seeing a hurt and healing it.

Tommy Barnette of the L.A. International Dream Center said that every great city needs a great church. I'd add that every great church needs a great children's ministry. If you will be the type of person who will see a need and meet it, your church will be full.

Find out what the needs of your kids are. Take them on a weekend retreat. Get to know them by hanging out with them. Give them a questionnaire to figure out their interests and needs. What cartoons do they watch? What percentage of those kids are dealing with their parents' divorces? What's important to your kids? That's where your vision is going to come from.

Early in my ministry I moved from a blue-collar church in Birmingham, Alabama, to a "yuppie" church in Montgomery, Alabama. When I made the move, I tried to bring a club program based on scouting with me. It didn't work.

One kid put it like this: "You want me to put down my computer to learn how to sharpen an axe?"

LARRY: *So you can't take some visions with you from one church to the next?*

> **Find out what the needs of your kids are.... That's where your vision is going to come from.**

JIM: That's right. I couldn't even shop the same way. At that blue-collar church I'd buy off-brand pop to save some money for my kids' events. I bought the same thing at the yuppie church, and I actually had a child approach me and ask if the church was experiencing financial problems. He offered to donate some money so we could buy some brand-name pop.

In fact, a big source of vision is to find out what's going on "in the house." Your job as an associate is to give your senior pastor what the pastor wants. Senior pastors are called to people groups and communities. Associate pastors are called to make the senior pastor's vision happen. That's a huge source of vision.

LARRY: *Any pitfalls that the budding visionary should avoid?*

JIM: "Thus saith the seminar speaker or the author" is going to cost you a lot of money. Look, every seminar speaker or author is where they are because at some point during their career, they heard from God themselves. Not every curriculum or philosophy is going to fit your church. Learn from these people, but you're going to have to hear God yourself.

how to be an effective director— whether you are one or not

Maybe you're a natural Director. Perhaps you've been trained to be strong in this area. Either way, this next section will help you achieve a personal Promised Land—you can increase your effectiveness as a Director.

And you non-Directors: Let's face it. In life, we sometimes have to do things we don't want to do. If I told my wife, "Sorry, the whole mechanical, handyman thing just isn't me," there'd be a huge price to pay.

Truth is, at times we need to broaden our range of skills for the sake of the dream. At home, that means occasionally I need to break out the power tools and hope for the best. In your children's ministry, you may have to step up and do things that don't feel quite like your calling—speaking to the church board or teaching the junior boys, for instance—but that need to be done.

> **Truth is, at times we need to broaden our range of skills for the sake of the dream.**

You, however, don't have to just *hope* for success. This how-to guide will break things down for you— step by step. You might not be a natural Director, but with hard work and determination, you'll soon be a convincing actor who can handle the role.

Keep in mind that I'm *not* talking about being inauthentic. If you're not a Director, you need to find one to involve in your ministry at some level. But until then, there's still some Director stuff to do—and you're going to have to do it.

This approach has worked for me. After 14 years, I can play a pretty convincing role as a Director. Truth be told, thinking like a director now comes naturally for me. I can vision cast with the best of them.

But it all started with *faking* it. Like Moses, I didn't feel like a visionary. I didn't think I had what it took to show up and cast a vision.

But that's what needed to be done, so I did it.

Here's how you can do it, too…

the directors' two-step dance

Directors lead from a two-part process: First they receive an Opening Night vision. Second, they communicate that vision to the whole group in such a way that the group is motivated to action.

Let's break this process down. We'll start by looking at how a director, or a leader wishing to grow some director-like skills, gains that Opening Night vision.

step one: find a vision

If you aren't a Director, you may wonder where those visions come from in the first place. Our culture has so glamorized the visionary leader that you might think grand visions come falling from the sky and land in the laps of these leaders. We picture lightning strikes, or a shaft of light piercing the clouds and spotlighting the leader, birthing new visions on impact.

Most Directors don't experience life this way. God can and does speak in an inescapable, revelatory way when he so pleases. If God wants to crack the sky and speak audibly to someone, I have no intention of telling that person God's not allowed to do that.

Many Directors *do* have sudden "aha!" moments that seem to spring from nowhere. But while the conscious awareness of an Opening Night vision often emerges full blown, that vision has often been percolating at the back of the Director's mind for some time.

Here are some common disciplines Directors practice to tune their hearts to a frequency that allows them to hear God's will for their children's ministry…

• Prayer

James 1:5-6 says, "If any of you lacks wisdom, he should ask God, who gives generously to all without fault, and it will be given to him. But when he asks, he must believe and not doubt, because he who doubts is like a wave of the sea, blown and tossed by the wind."

Listing prayer as a resource for discovering the Promised Land is so obvious that it's almost silly to mention it. Think about it: God is madly in love with the church. The church was founded by the blood of his own Son. Why *wouldn't* leaders in the church be listening to God?

When God is approached by a Director whose heart is submitted to God, who is begging for the wisdom to know how to make the church more beautiful, what do you *think* God is going to do? Be coy, resentful, or distant? Absolutely not! James says God gives wisdom generously to those who ask for it.

A Director cultivates an Opening Night vision by being in a constant dialogue with God. "Where do you want me to lead these people?" needs to be a Director's daily prayer.

But…is it?

Is the discipline of listening in prayer part of your daily life? Do you regularly block off days to fast, meditate, and listen to God?

If not, how will you hear the Opening Night vision that God wants to share with you? God generously gives vision to leaders who make a lifestyle of asking for it, but there's no biblical promise that God will bully his way through your busyness and inflict it on you.

> **A Director cultivates an Opening Night vision by being in a constant dialogue with God.**

How can you possibly know you're doing what God wants you to do—and pointing your ministry in the direction God desires—unless your Opening Night vision is first birthed in prayer?

• Studying God's Word

One way Directors gain vision is to comb Scriptures looking for direction as to what God wants their ministries to become.

Part of my children's ministry vision was born out of a personal study on the children and youth in the Bible who did great things for God.

The Bible is filled with pint-sized heroes who did amazing things for God. An unnamed girl captured during a raid the Assyrian Army launched against Israel was forced to be the slave of Naaman, an Assyrian general. The girl had every reason to hate her captor. Instead, she shared God's love with Naaman and referred him to Elijah, who could heal his leprosy. One of the first international missionaries in the Bible was a minor, and *she* didn't need a whale to convince her to share her faith with her enemies.

David, of course, defended God's honor on the battlefield. Ishmael moved God to action through his prayers.

Samuel listened to God's voice and prophesied against a corrupt priesthood.

Paul's nephew disrupted a clandestine assassination plot against his uncle.

Stories of these children and adolescents filled me with a vision for creating a ministry in which children could view themselves as disciples and servants.

That vision is played out in many ways, the most current Opening Night vision being our "Can Do Kids" program. On Wednesdays kids flock to the church not to be entertained, but to be servants.

> **Directors are detectives who look for clues as to what God is trying to accomplish with this generation of children.**

They're trained in puppetry. They create "Kid Made Movies" that are used in children's church on Sunday morning. These "Can Do Kids" host all-church prayer meetings, visit a neighboring nursing home, clean preschool toys, and perform a host of other meaningful service projects.

It all started with a Bible study I did years ago. That study sparked an Opening Night vision in me that still has an ironclad hold on my imagination. I'm positive that those verses about children will never release their hold on me.

• Studying other healthy and thriving children's ministries

Effective Directors study other children's ministries. They find out what's working and why. It just makes sense to look for examples of what God is already blessing. In his book *Experiencing God,* Henry Blackaby describes this principle as, "Find out what God is already doing and join it."

Directors are detectives who look for clues as to what God is trying to accomplish with this generation of children. A smart Director will turn to other Directors who have already heard from God.

Directors network with other ministries in their area. They attend conferences and training events. They read books written by seasoned children's ministry leaders. Directors comb the Web and listen to training tapes to make themselves aware of potential Promised Land opportunities.

A caution: Some leaders who study other programs resort to what I call "cutting and pasting." They try to lift a program from a thriving ministry and install it in their own churches, without first understanding the principles behind the program.

That's like transplanting an organ into a patient without first making sure there's a blood type and tissue match. Slap the wrong kidney into a recipient and the recipient will reject the kidney, ending up in even worse shape. The organ and recipient must be compatible.

Let me give you an example. From time to time I'm pressured to install a midweek club program in our church that emphasizes giving kids rewards for rote Scripture memorization and winning competitive games. It's a popular club. Thousands of churches use it and draw large crowds of kids.

You might even be using this club with great success.

I've got nothing against this club, but I'll never allow it to be installed in our children's ministry.

Why? Because the program and our church aren't compatible.

This club emphasizes competition. We value teamwork. This club majors in kids being able to place a verse in their short-term memory. We major in children comprehending and applying Scripture. If I installed this club on Wednesdays, I'd lose my learning lab for the kids to discover their gifts and talents.

A few years ago, a senior leader in the church pressured me to launch this program. I politely told him that it sounded like a good first initiative for the new children's pastor.

My point? There are many successful programs and curriculums. Each one has a "blood type"—a set of beliefs and values about education and discipleship. You can't mix and match these programs without realizing that you are performing surgery—surgery that *will* affect the health and unity of your ministry.

Look to other churches for principles, methods, and God-sightings. *Don't* cut and paste until you know there is a blood-type match.

• Study your "Big Church"

Directors in children's ministry often rocket around the country, grabbing nuggets from conferences, without ever stopping to ask, "What has God *already* revealed to the senior leadership in my church?"

Here's a bold statement that might not sit well with you at first glance: No children's ministry has the right to operate as an independent entity from the Big Church. Your children's ministry has a responsibility to reflect the Promised Land concept and values of your larger church.

Not sure you agree with that? Consider…

• Craig Jutila modeled his All-Stars children's curriculum on the Purpose-Driven model that defines Saddleback Church where Craig is children's minister. Every child leaves Craig's program understanding the Five Purposes of the church and the concept of "running the bases"—the church's metaphor for growing as a disciple.

• Shortly after Sue Miller joined the staff at Willow Creek Community Church as Children's Ministry Director, the children's ministry began reflecting the shape of the adult ministries. Willow Creek is known for its large weekend services and massive small-group ministry. Willow Creek places a high premium on harnessing the power of the arts to communicate the gospel.

When you look to *your* "Big Church" as a source of vision, power is unleashed.

Miller installed a large group/small group model called Promiseland that allows children to experience the power of a large corporate experience and the intimacy of a small group—all within an hour. Promiseland works because it reflects the vision that helped birth the church.

When you look to *your* "Big Church" as a source of vision, power is unleashed. Children leave your ministry philosophically prepared for a lifetime of serving in your church. It feels familiar to them. They already know where they can make a contribution.

It works the other direction, too. Adult volunteers entering your children's ministry already understand how your ministry is wired.

Imagine the power in that! When your Promised Land concept

mirrors the Promised Land Concept of your Big Church, there's synergy. There's a common approach to and understanding of where you're going. Plus, there's leverage when budget time rolls around and you approach senior leadership asking for funds to support *their* goals.

As you look to your Big Church for vision, study its vision statement, core values, and strategic plan. Take your senior leader to lunch, and don't ask for *anything*. Simply encourage your leader to share his or her dreams about where God could take your church. Then ask God how you can lead your ministry to help your entire church make it to the Promised Land.

If you're a Director reading this and you're thinking, "But I have a completely *different* Promised Land concept than the senior leadership of my church does," I've got some pointed advice for you:

Either align your ministry with the Big Church, or get out.

You're in danger of being that mismatched organ I talked about earlier. If you're convinced yours is the right vision for your church's children's ministry, then God is prompting you to move on. Sharpen your résumé. It's quite possible you have the right vision, but you're in the wrong place.

If you stay, you'll only sow seeds of discontent and confusion.

• Study your volunteers

A wise Director studies his or her volunteer base as a source for vision. Children's pastors who show up at a new church and immediately impose a new vision are either rookies or fools.

When I came to my current ministry, I managed to prove I was both.

Paul writes that God gave church leaders "for the equipping of the saints for the work of service, for the building up of the body of Christ" (Ephesians 4:12, NASB). That means, Directors, that God carefully selected the people that he gave you to equip. God called those people to your ministry and equipped them with gifts to use in ministry. Wise Directors understand that God has *already* given you the resources to accomplish the Opening Night vision he desires to see implemented in your church.

What does this mean, practically speaking?

If you're tone deaf and God hasn't given you a single volunteer who has musical talent, then God probably doesn't expect you to have a Promised Land vision of creating a kid's worship album.

God isn't cruel, and he doesn't give cookie-cutter visions. Perhaps you're *loaded* with volunteers who are good with their hands and who have practical skills. Perhaps your Promised Land concept should be a mentoring program that uses adults to train kids in carpentry, sewing, and crafts.

God hides parts of the Opening Night vision in the hearts of your core volunteers. You can unearth these clues by actively getting to know your volunteers, serving them, and listening to them.

Tap these five sources of vision to help you find God's Opening Night picture for your children's ministry. But be warned: This isn't an easy undertaking. Visions aren't crafted from start to finish at a weekend leadership retreat.

Build these five sources of vision into your ministry as a *lifestyle*. Only then will you discover the Opening Night concept that God has in mind for your children's ministry.

But mark my words: It's worth the effort.

You've received and identified an Opening Night vision. Now it's time to do the second step in the Director's dance: Share the vision.

step two: sharing your vision

So you have a vision. Your Opening Night vision literally keeps you up at night. Every time you think about your vision, your heart pumps faster. If you're a Director, you can relate to this notion: You can almost *taste* how the vision will look when it's complete.

There's just one thing between you and actualizing your dream: No one else cares.

Your volunteers don't care. Your pastor doesn't care. That annoying guy who counts every penny in the church budget doesn't care. Your spouse doesn't care. Why? *Because you haven't shared your vision yet.*

Nothing happens until *your* vision becomes *their* vision.

It's not enough if your volunteers and bosses simply tolerate your vision. They need to climb so far on board that they're along for the ride too. Your leadership and team need to be willing to invest their leadership styles, gifts, and talents into making your vision come to life.

The problem is that people don't lay their lives down for someone else's vision. People will make sacrifices only for their *own* priorities. You need to tell your Opening Night idea in such a compelling manner that people around you adopt it as their own. It's time to share your vision, but first you need to decide who needs to hear it…and who needs to hear it *first*.

The first people on the list need to be…

1. Those whose approval you need.

To whom are you accountable? A pastor? An elder board? You need to get the buy-in from the leaders in your life for your Opening Night vision.

> **People don't lay their lives down for someone else's vision. People will make sacrifices only for their *own* priorities.**

Here's a rule of thumb: The bigger the Opening Night, the more support you'll need from the top. That's true even if you work in a church where you're afforded a great deal of autonomy in shaping the children's ministry.

The goal is to plant and nurture your God-given vision for the ministry in the hearts and minds of people who write your budget…who can protect you if opposition arises…who can carry on and implement the vision even if you leave.

Communicate the vision to your leaders. That's part of being a good follower.

2. Those who'll be doing the work.

Since you're a Director and not a dictator, you need to build the team who'll actually give the time, talent, and effort to get the job done. Reality check: no matter how effective a Director you are, you can't do it alone.

Write out your Opening Night vision. Then make a short list of what sort of people are needed to see the vision through to reality. If you have a team member with the Production Assistant leadership style, ask that person to help you with this. Especially if you scored low in the Production Assistant style, you'll need a second set of eyes to create lists.

3. Cheerleaders and curmudgeons.

Your church is filled with opinion-shapers. They may not hold any official title, but they're quick to form strong opinions and share those opinions with everyone they know.

Cheerleaders and curmudgeons create public opinion on any issue about which they're passionate. If you leave them out of the loop, they'll fill in the blanks themselves—loudly.

Share your Opening Night vision with each group. Cheerleaders will then help you generate buzz among the ranks. They'll provide energy and enthusiasm.

Curmudgeons may not be enthusiastic, but if you listen to them you'll discover the weaknesses in your plan and be better prepared to handle opposition. Meet with cheerleaders regularly and a curmudgeon only once; it's not a good use of time trying to lead someone who will never follow you. The most you'll ever win from a curmudgeon is mutual understanding and a live-and-let-live truce. Let that be enough.

> **Cheerleaders and curmudgeons create public opinion on any issue about which they're passionate.**

Once you've secured the support of your leadership, emerging team, and informed the opinion makers, it's time to go public and tell others.

4. Tell your other volunteers.

The people who make children's ministry happen deserve to hear significant children's ministry information early on, even if they aren't directly involved in your new Opening Night vision. By communicating with them early in the process, you demonstrate that you understand their importance and value. You also may discover that a handful of your volunteers are willing to increase their commitment and pitch in with the new initiative. The chances that any of your teams will feel neglected also diminish.

You have just so much energy to go around. As you invest in the new Opening Night vision, you're in danger of shortchanging some of your existing teams. When you keep everyone informed, you reduce that risk.

5. The congregation.

Once you've won the support of your bosses, your teams, and the influence shapers, it's now time to go public. Get the word out to the congregation, *especially* parents whose children may be impacted.

how to communicate your vision

A new vision, or even an old vision newly embraced, is going to bring about change. That requires you to be intentional about communicating clearly, concisely, and often.

Directors, here's how to communicate your vision so it takes hold in the hearts of others:

• One-on-One Meetings

Schedule these meetings with key leaders and volunteers. One-on-one meetings are time consuming, but over lunch or a cup of coffee you can share your heart. You'll not only communicate your vision, but giving of your time also communicates that you value their opinion.

• Training Meetings

Use scheduled teacher-training meetings to cast the vision for existing staff. Use staff meetings, if you're on a church staff, to accomplish the same thing.

• The Pulpit

Be sure that there's at least one mention of children's ministry each month from the pulpit. And don't assume that sermons are the only way to keep children's ministry vision in front of people. Testimonies, skits, and celebrations of events are great ways to keep children's ministry in the public eye.

• Field Trips

Take a small team of leaders and parents to a church that embodies your Opening Night vision. Do you have a dream of an attractively and creatively decorated children's ministry space that grabs kids' imagination the moment kids arrive? Find a church that's already created a 3-D environment.

Another rule of thumb for communicating vision: Only resort to talking about a vision when you can't show it. Some people need to *see* something before they can buy in.

• Become the Vision

Do you have an Opening Night vision of your teachers trading in their tired teaching methods for active learning methods? Use active learning methods yourself when you train your volunteers. Become the poster child for what an actualized vision looks like in your church.

• Use Testimonies

Do you want to cast a vision of your ministry being known for welcoming visitors? Videotape the story of a new family coming to your community and your church. Have them talk about how it felt to try to connect with other people in your church.

> Jump-start the buzz by getting your kids excited. Excited kids translate into informed parents.

• Children's Church

The kids are your congregation. Jump-start the buzz by getting your kids excited. Excited kids translate into informed parents.

So there you have it—how to act like a Director. Follow these pointers and you're well on your way to providing your children's ministry with an energizing vision. Let me leave you with two thoughts as we close this chapter.

First, remember there are no shortcuts for being a Director. You *need* to truly hear from God. That can be hard, lonely work.

Second, once you have heard from God, know that God offers you the same promise he extended to Moses. "Now then go, and I, even I,

will be with your mouth, and teach you what you are to say" (Exodus 4:12, NASB).

Every part of the Director's task, hearing and saying, is filled with God.

a director's prayer

Dear God,

You give me glimpses into the future and allow me to see what our children's ministry could be if we put our faith in you. Thank you for this insight.

God, I pray for pure vision—don't let me "fuzz up" my sight with sinful habits or pride. Give me the ability to share these pictures of the future with the team. Make me persuasive but not manipulative.

Help me give energy to our team to courageously press into the future. However, God, help me to not ignore the demands of the present.

In Jesus' name, amen.

for reflection and discussion

1. Does your team currently enjoy the services of a God-honoring Director? If so, what returns have you seen? If not, who in your congregation could you recruit to join your team?

2. What sources of vision does your children's ministry currently mine? What are some untapped sources of vision for your children's ministry?

CHAPTER (4)

the **production assistant**

Debbie cringed when the phone rang. *"More bad news," she muttered as she lifted the receiver. The telephone had rung off the hook all week with frustrating calls about the musical.*

First, the choir director had phoned to let Debbie know in no uncertain terms that the choir would continue to practice in the sanctuary on Wednesday nights—period. Debbie hadn't checked the schedule before announcing that rehearsals for the children's musical would be on Wednesday nights—a major tactical error. Debbie could barely interrupt the choir director long enough get an apology out.

Pastor Jack made the next call. He was surprised to learn that the musical was happening at all. A particularly cranky trustee had ambushed Jack at a board meeting and pointed out that the musical wasn't in the budget. The trustee demanded to know what the musical would cost. Jack tried to be polite, but his irritation bled through. He'd given Debbie permission to do research, not plunge ahead and commit funds.

When pressed, Debbie had to admit she had no idea how much it cost to produce a musical. She promised to raise the funds, though she had no idea how.

The next series of phone calls came from "concerned" parents. Apparently, some parents were already jockeying to land lead roles for their kids.

Mrs. Jones' daughter had participated in the local youth theater for three years, so Mrs. Jones fully expected her Emily to be handed the lead—whatever it was. After all, Emily had more theater experience than the other children combined.

Three parents called to complain about Mrs. Jones' presumption and imperious tone. Other parents phoned to find out how auditions would be conducted. Debbie fended off parents by promising to get back to them within a week's time.

So naturally, Debbie's heart sank when she heard the phone ring again. It was Patricia.

"Debbie, we need to talk. Things aren't going well with this musical."

Debbie felt her defenses shoot up as Patricia referred to the phone calls Debbie had fielded all week. "Why is Patricia in the middle of all this gossip?"

Debbie mused that Patricia was never fully behind the musical. Every time Debbie pumped the team up with enthusiasm, Patricia seemed to follow behind and deflate the momentum by bursting the bubble with detail-oriented questions. "That's it. I'm calling Patricia out once and for all, "Debbie decided with a flash of anger.

Fortunately, Patricia spoke first.

"I think I can help with the musical," Patricia said. "I can't act or run a light board, but I think I can create some order here. Look, I know you get frustrated when I don't respond to your 'Rah! Rah!' cheerleading stuff.

"It's just that I'm busy thinking about how to get things done. I don't know how to explain it, but whenever people share big ideas, I start to create a mental road map of how to get there. I've kept my mouth shut because I didn't want you to think that I'm challenging your leadership. On the other hand, all the chaos I'm seeing is frustrating me.

"So here's my offer: I'll be your Production Assistant. You're the boss. You give me the big picture, and I'll create a map that everyone can follow. Together, we'll get this musical done."

Debbie was stung by what she heard. Create order? Chaos? Is that what Patricia thought she was seeing? Why, if people would just get behind the project instead of slowing everything down with questions, they'd…they'd…

Debbie sighed. Patricia had a point. Despite all Debbie's efforts to generate energy and create a sense of urgency, people were see-ing…well, chaos. Debbie swallowed hard.

"Uh, yeah. That would be a good thing. Let's get together and do lunch."

Debbie sunk into the couch, nursing the embarrassment of ad-mitting her weakness to Patricia. On the other hand, Debbie knew that things would be getting better soon.

profile of a production assistant

In theater, a Production Assistant works closely with the Director to help the Director shepherd the cast to their goal. The Production Assistant develops the master calendars—the rehearsal schedules, ad-vertising schedules, and set design schedules.

In a ministry context, the Production Assistant determines where the ministry is at this moment, then creates a map to where the Director's Opening Night vision would place the ministry. The Production Assistant lays out a series of well-defined and logically progressing steps.

Think of it this way: The Director points to the horizon and shouts,

learning the parts If you think you might be a Production Assistant, reread the "Profile of a Production Assistant" again, this time with a highlighter pen in hand. The profile is a composite description of Production Assistants in general, but you know yourself best.

Customize the profile to fit yourself. Highlight sentences that your spouse or friends would point to and say, "Oh, yeah—that's you. No question about it!" Place a star next to sentences that don't describe you at all.

If you know you *aren't* a Production Assistant, decide if you have a Production Assistant in your life. Does this description remind you of anyone in your church or children's ministry? Jot down the names of those people below.

_____

_____

_____

_____

"Promised Land ahead!" The Production Assistant lays down the train track that will carry the children's ministry to that Promised Land in an orderly and harmonious manner.

The Director generates electricity. The Production Assistant focuses the energy and points it the right direction.

The Production Assistant creates this order by developing calendars, timelines, and to-do lists that measure the children's ministry's progress as it moves toward its goals. Leaders with a Production Assistant Leadership Style quickly break large projects into a series of manageable steps. Production Assistants quickly identify what resources, volunteers, and budgets need to be in place in order to lead the children's ministry through change in an orderly fashion. The Production Assistant is a master of managing organizational change.

A skilled Production Assistant knows that objectives and tasks aren't the only "freight" that needs to be moved down the track. There's also a need to manage the changes in "buy-in" and public opinion. A skilled Production Assistant is able to identify how team-mates and influential people in the congregation feel about the Opening Night vision, and to guide the Director in connecting with the right people at the right time.

The Production Assistant enjoys being valued and needed by the Director as a trusted resource and confidant. Production Assistants feel most valuable to their teams when their skills are used to help a team move through change efficiently and with minimal conflict.

Production Assistants understand that managing change isn't just about moving the ball down the field. It's also about taking care of the people involved.

Production Assistants are frustrated by leaders who initiate change before taking the time to think through the implications of that change. Directors who suddenly deviate from an agreed-upon plan are also a source of frustration, no matter how well-intended the Director may have been.

A common weakness in Production Assistants is a lack of flexibility. A rigid Production Assistant can mistake a Director's creativity, brainstorming, or adaptation as cavalier or undisciplined behavior.

> **Production Assistants understand that managing change isn't just about moving the ball down the field.**

It's crucial that the Director and Production Assistant enjoy a close relationship in which they are able to tell each other the whole truth. The entire children's ministry benefits when that relationship is strong.

Production Assistants must realize they live in a world where no plan is ever executed exactly as drafted. Volunteers adapt, personalize, or ignore parts of the plan as the volunteers do their part in moving the ministry toward the Promised Land. It's not unusual for a Production Assistant to miss the beauty of a detour because he or she is busy pointing out that the map wasn't followed.

And that's at the heart of the dilemma faced by Production Assistants: They care about the people involved, but they also care deeply about their planning. It's a position of strength if the Production Assistant balances the values, and a danger if the Production Assistant becomes too task focused.

Production Assistants are embodiments of the second leadership star: Providing road maps. Production Assistants are brilliant at shaping strategic plans. They also are very capable of supporting heart-healthy ministries and providing enormous muscle.

Some Opening Night concepts are so large that it's hard for team members to see that they're making progress. The measurable objectives provided by Production Assistants help volunteers see progress, and that provides enormous motivation to the team.

Bible case study of a production assistant: SOLOMON

King Solomon is an example of a high-level leader who spoke primarily in a Production Assistant voice. However, in spite of Solomon's storied wisdom, he made some key mistakes in process management that eventually contributed to the unraveling of his kingdom.

Solomon's father, David, was known for being a fierce warrior who conquered Israel's enemies. Solomon inherited an Israel that was respected as a power by the international community. In fact, Egypt thought it was in their best interest to enter a marriage alliance with Solomon early in his administration (1 Kings 3:1-3).

Solomon used Israel's favorable position to begin extensive building projects throughout the country. These projects highlighted his skills and shortcomings as a process leader.

First, Solomon began the construction of the temple. His father, David, had the vision for building the temple, but God didn't allow David's involvement. So David purchased the land, collected much of the building materials, and made an agreement with the King of Tyre to supply workers and cedar timber.

It was Solomon, however, who developed a seven-year calendar to get the building project accomplished.

First Solomon appointed Huram, a Phoenician contractor, to supervise the work.[1] Solomon instructed Huram to design a Temple that reflected the design of the tabernacle, the portable place of worship, which had been designed during the days of Moses.

Next was the issue of labor. The King of Tyre supplied artisans as part of his contract with Solomon. However, the labor demands were far greater. Solomon conscripted 30,000 workers for the project. Laborers had to work one out of every three months on the temple project.

Since the building of the temple took so long, Solomon devised a plan to minimize the impact of the project on the people of Jerusalem. To reduce noise pollution, Solomon instructed that every stone of the temple be precut at the rock quarries, outside of Jerusalem (1 Kings 6:7).

First Kings and 1 Chronicles describe the temple as an ornate and expensive building. In fact, some interior walls and cedar beams were gold-plated (1 Kings 6:15, 18). Part of Solomon's challenge in this building project was in the financing.

Solomon's road map for his temple's capital campaign was levying a system of taxes. Solomon divided the 10 northern tribes into 12 districts. Each district was ruled by a governor whose job was to collect food for Solomon and his court for one month out of the year (1 Kings 4:7-12). Some of that food was shipped to the King of Tyre as payment for his services in the temple project (1 Kings 5:10-11).

Apparently, this building project—like most—cost more than originally budgeted.

Apparently, this building project—like most—cost more than originally budgeted. Cash flow became a serious issue. Solomon gave 20 towns in Galilee to Hiram as collateral for a loan of 120 talents of gold (1 Kings 9:11-14). For all of Solomon's planning, he was unable to accurately anticipate the financial impact of a project this large.

Solomon needed a new plan to increase his wealth. So he built a fleet of ships to engage in international trade (1 Kings 9:26-28). Solomon's fleet embarked on a three-year journey to Ophir, a trading port, and returned with 420 talents of gold.

Solomon's planning paid off! The cash flow problem was solved. Second Chronicles 8:1-2 suggests that Solomon was able to purchase these cities back when his gold reserves returned to a healthy level.

Due to shrewd planning, Solomon was able to both remedy his financial crisis and position himself to take on new building projects after the temple was completed.

Seven years after construction began, the temple was completed. Second Chronicles 5–7 tells about an extravagant celebration that took place to dedicate the temple. The dedication ceremony was a powerful, unifying event that galvanized the nation's commitment to worshipping God.

Solomon's road map to accomplishing David's vision of building a house of worship worked. Mission accomplished.

Unfortunately, fatal flaws in Solomon's road map didn't account for leading the hearts of his people. Solomon's policy of exempting the tribes of Judah and Benjamin from being conscripted into forced labor and taxes was extremely unpopular and created resentment.

Solomon's road map had built an emotional divide between the northern and southern tribes that was irreparable. Later, when God judged Solomon for his idolatry, the kingdom splintered exactly on the fault lines that Solomon had built.

for discussion and reflection

1. Financial pressures forced Solomon to revise his original road map for the construction of the temple. What lessons do you think this story teaches us about how we handle our road maps? How do you feel when you are forced to leave your original plans?

2. What were the prices that Solomon had to pay for ignoring the emotional impact that his plan had on his people? How can your team make sure that it's in touch with the hearts of your volunteers, parents, and children?

case study: michael bonner

Michael Bonner is pastor of Family Ministries at Westlake Bible Church in Austin, Texas. He's been involved in children's ministry since 1997. Michael took the Dramatic Leadership Assessment Test and scored high in both the Director and Production Assistant styles. I asked Michael to describe a time in his ministry when he had to lead his volunteers through a change process.

"At my first church in Dallas, Texas, I had a vision for a creative children's ministry—one that used drama and music to communicate God's Word. However, it was a traditional church where the children sat in desks and quietly listened to teachers lecture.

"I didn't rush the change. For the first year, I took my team on six field trips to study other children's ministries. My team just observed, and I was careful not to editorialize. I never told my team what to expect before any of the field trips.

"After each field trip, I'd let my team debrief and discuss their impressions of the morning. They had permission to say anything.

"A fun thing happened midway through the field trips: The team became more tolerant of creative teaching experiences. The majority of the group rated the first churches as radical or extreme. However, as the visiting schedule progressed, they viewed these churches as average. Their calibrations changed."

> **"I didn't rush the change. For the first year, I took my team on six field trips to study other children's ministries."**

Michael's team was finally ready for change, so Michael assessed his ministry's facilities and budget. Financially, he was set. His budget could accommodate an "arts-driven" ministry.

Facilities were another story.

The church had an amphitheater perfect for staging dramas. However, other staff members were using the amphitheater. Michael needed to develop a plan to transition the stage between services so both departments could use the space.

The next step was to prepare his team for the emotional experience of change. Michael brought in a potter to do a demonstration of the

michael bonner's tips for leading teams through change

• Know your own attitudes toward change.
Michael knows that he has a high tolerance for change.

"You tend to migrate toward people who think like you do and reject the perspectives of team members who take in change slower than you do. That's a dangerous place to be," says Michael.

• Know every team member's tolerance for change.
"People are all over the curve when it comes to adopting change," notes Michael. "You need to find the middle of the curve and lead from there so you can bring the stragglers along."

Michael describes his wife as being slow to take in change. "It's a great asset. My wife gets me to look at a proposed change through other people's eyes. That keeps me out of a lot of trouble."

• Address the root problems.
Michael advises against dealing only with surface issues.

"It's important to figure out what is at the root of the resistance. Anger is called a secondary emotion. The key is figuring out *why* there's anger, why there's resistance to change. *That's* where you lead. Not at the symptoms level."

• Allow people to protest.
"If people know they are genuinely being heard, they are more willing to come along with the change," says Michael.

• Be willing to fire someone.
"At a church I pastored in Ohio, I implemented a new security policy," recalls Michael. "I had a volunteer who simply refused to sign a release so I could do a background check on her. The whole process was insulting to her.

"After a team meeting where I laid out the whys of the policy, and a one-on-one meeting, I finally had to give her a deadline to get the background check done. She called my bluff, so I had to fire her.

"If someone simply won't come along, it's time to release him or her from your team."

process of making a vase on her wheel. After the presentation, Michael explained to his team that they would be feeling pressure during their change process, much like the clay felt pressure as it was being molded by the potter.

The experience caught the attention of Michael's volunteer staff. The next day, Michael received several phone calls from volunteers wondering exactly what kind of pressures they would be feeling.

Next Michael had to show his team how he wanted their church to look. He led the children's church for two weeks and had tight controls over every detail of the morning. It wasn't enough to *tell* his people what he wanted. He had to *show* them.

Michael then met with his team to debrief how those two weeks went. He allowed team members to vent their frustrations and concerns over the new program. Michael used their input to make a midcourse correction and build in an evaluation that helped team members know if the children were "getting it."

The change process had occurred. Michael's team owned the vision of reaching children through the creative arts, and they began to run the remodeled ministry on their own, *as* their own.

Did Michael successfully lead everyone through the change process? Absolutely not. Some volunteers resisted the change throughout the whole process. Michael notes, "It's important to recognize that no matter how much planning you do, you won't successfully bring everyone through the change process."

One of Michael's key volunteers *refused* to participate in the field trips. One couple disagreed with the changes but kept trying to stay involved. They would take the new lessons and try to bend them back into the old format.

"You're not going to hit a home run every time. Not everyone will come along. When I made this change, all I could see was the one or two naysayers. I couldn't see the hundred happy people cheering us on. It's tough to be in the middle of that. You need to step back and look at the big picture. You can't let a handful of people bring you down."

> **"You're not going to hit a home run every time. Not everyone will come along."**

69

how to be a production assistant—whether you are one or not

Whether you are a *natural* Production Assistant looking to sharpen your skills, or someone who just needs to *behave* like a Production Assistant, here's your step-by-step guide to success.

But maybe the idea of *behaving* like something you're not makes you wonder if I'm asking you to be a fake.

In a sense that's exactly what I'm asking you to do.

A few years ago I started taking tae kwon do classes with my son. When I started training, I was faking every move I made. *Nothing* came naturally. The strikes, the hits, the stances—they were all new (and painful).

I watched the black belts to see what they were doing and then mimicked them—I faked it.

After three years of faking it, *I'm* now a black belt.

The point of this story: The engine of "becoming" is "behavior." If you're a natural Production Assistant who wants to be a world class Production Assistant, you start by *acting* like a world class Production Assistant.

If you're looking to compliment a different style by adding some Production Assistant skills, you start by *behaving* like a Production Assistant. The skills will develop as you go.

The first step to "becoming" is "behaving."

Let's get started.

1. Identify the Conflict

Every Promised Land vision has conflict bound up into it if for no other reason than you're moving a ministry from right here to over there. Plus, there's selling the notion that the grass really *is* greener on the other side of the fence. It's also stickier because it's covered with milk and honey.

As a Production Assistant, part of your job is to manage conflict and bring order out of chaos. Those are handy skills to have, and they develop with practice.

Here's the thing about conflict and change: If you expect to make

big changes, you can expect to see big conflicts. If you tackle only changes that won't ruffle feathers, they'll probably be negligible changes.

Consider Debbie's Promised Land. She wants to stage a musical, but in reality she isn't *just* producing a musical. There's not a whole lot of conflict in staging a musical.

Debbie's real conflict is that she wants to transform children into missionaries.

Do you see the difference? Knocking off a musical is just work. It's *not* terribly inspiring. Turning kids into missionaries, on the other hand, has a huge amount of conflict bound up in it.

Debbie doesn't see what all the conflict is about, but Patricia does. She sees there's conflict, and she's committed to figuring out what steps she can take to resolve the conflict and chaos. She'll quickly uncover the deeper, more meaningful conflicts.

If you're a Production Assistant and you don't see any conflict in changes that a Director is initiating, sit down and talk with the Director. He or she may not understand all the conflicts, but you can bet there have been calls or comments made that contain nuggets of the conflict. Probe so the conflicts are discovered sooner rather than later.

2. Identify Assets and Barriers

Once you're certain where you are and where you want to be, it's time to audit your ministry and discover what needs to change to make it to the Promised Land.

What resources will be required to build that bridge or march over that mountain?

What are your assets—people, programs, and things—that move you toward the Promised Land?

What are the barriers you'll need to cross? What resources will be required to build that bridge or march over that mountain?

Pay special attention during your audit to...

• Budget and Supplies

This is a critical element of your planning and map-making. What money and resources do you need to make it to your Promised Land?

Revisiting our story, Patricia needs to get a picture of what it costs to produce a musical. She'll need to price props, costumes, practice tapes, songbooks, and volunteer appreciation gifts. Since this event wasn't in the church budget, Patricia will need to develop a fund-raising plan to provide the resources.

And if you have any doubts about the importance of the Production Assistant role, consider: What will happen if Patricia *doesn't* do all that? The wheels will fall off the production in record time.

• Facilities

Do your facilities support your ministry's Promised Land vision?

Suppose your Director has a dream of hosting an outreach event for 200 elementary-aged children. Do you have room to host that many kids?

Production Assistants *know* better than to trust Directors to fill out the room reservation forms.

When Production Assistants deal with Directors, the Production Assistants must always ask themselves, "What if this crazy dream actually works? Are we ready for success?"

If your church can't support an event for 200, develop a plan to secure facilities that *can* accommodate the event, and update your budget accordingly.

Production Assistants are the ones who check the policies and double-check the church calendar to make sure rooms are available when the Director needs them.

And Production Assistants *know* better than to trust Directors to fill out the room reservation forms.

• Technology

Look at your Promised Land concept and make sure you have the technology to pull it off. Do you need a publishing software package so you can create a newsletter? What about CD players, microphones, PA systems, or DVD players? Does your church have the technology in hand, or will you need to rent or borrow the equipment? Do you need to schedule the church's A/V tech to help you?

Production Assistants ask those questions before it's too late to switch to a plan B.

• The Cast

How many volunteers will you need to get to the Promised Land? What *kinds* of volunteers will you need—teachers, sound techs, chaperones?

Production Assistants look at every task that needs to be accomplished and identify who'll do it. Then they draft a simple job description for each position. The busy, competent people you want to add to your team will want to know exactly what's expected of them before they sign up for the task.

• Values

Assessing values is admittedly a subjective task. Yet, it's a task that's required for a leadership team if that team intends to initiate or manage change.

For instance, let's suppose you want to install a Volunteer Screening Policy in your children's ministry that requires every volunteer to undergo a criminal background check. Let's say that your church has been established for 70 years. There's never been a problem of a volunteer doing anything improper.

Your Director begins to share her vision of the screening policy, and several of the "old guard" Sunday School teachers begin to resent the policy. They become indignant over the perceived lack of trust. They see the church as an intimate, happy family where everyone loves and trusts each other.

What's the problem? These volunteers lack the value that the church needs to be a safe place for visitors to explore their faith journey. Visitors *don't* trust a new church where they don't know a soul. When the Production Assistant draws the road map, that map needs to include time for the Director and the Drama Coach to shape the team's values before the change is initiated.

• Skills

In a five-star, excellent theatrical production, there's top-notch acting. And at that level you'll discover that most of the actors have worked with a drama coach or done class work that helped them develop their acting chops. The actors have more than raw talent; they have developed skills, too.

Revisit your Opening Night vision. What kind of talents and knowledge will your volunteers require? An awareness of policies and procedures? Teaching skills? Relational abilities?

Discover who on your leadership team has Drama Coach abilities (see Chapter 6 for more about Drama Coaches), and determine what training the team needs in order to pull off an excellent Opening Night.

3. Build a Calendar

This is where Production Assistants shine. They're able to map out a process to get from where they are to where they want to be, and to do it with a calendar, a timeline, or another tool that lets them outline manageable, doable steps to plant your team squarely in the Promised Land.

Think of that journey as a two-act play.

Act One begins with "Act One, Scene One: Where You are Today" and ends with "Act One, Last Scene: A Good Night's Sleep Before Opening Night."

Why a good night's sleep? Because by mapping out what needs to happen and following the map, everything is in great shape. All the details are nailed down; everything is in place. All that's left is what comes in Act Two.

Act Two contains everything else—but you've mapped that all out, too.

Consider the following chart.

Act One	Act Two
• Vision Casting • Promoting • Budgeting/Fund Raising • Securing Facilities • Securing Technology • Recruiting • Training • "A Good Night's Sleep Before Opening Night"	• Opening Night • Clean Up • Next Steps • Appreciation • Evaluation

Notice that this chart is just a general outline—there's room for lots of detail to fit into each of the headings. Plus, the Production Assistant will add calendar dates next to each task.

Do you naturally think in terms of linear steps and time-lines? A natural Production Assistant does, and it's a leadership function that's necessary if your children's ministry is going to move forward. It's the only way you can get everyone on the same page.

If God didn't wire you to naturally be a Production Assistant, that doesn't remove the need to have this leadership function on your team. Be sure you have a Production Assistant in place—or prepare to fake these skills until they become second nature to you. You may never be completely comfortable with the Production Assistant role, but you can fulfill at least some of it.

Let's say your Opening Night concept is a "Back to School Party" designed to generate enthusiasm for the new children's ministry year, and to provide an orientation for new kids who started attending during your summer outreach.

The Production Assistant will get the party's date on the church calendar, then begin building the schedule from *both* directions from that date.

Before the party there will be a plan for creating the program, assembling the needed resources, and addressing invitation postcards to first-time visitors.

After the party there will be time for cleanup, sending thank-you notes to volunteers, and meeting with the team to evaluate the party. Production Assistants will also take notes from the evaluation and file them away for next year.

Skilled Production Assistants bring order to the multitude of tasks that take place in every ministry, but they do so in a way that's "actor" and "audience" friendly. They control the pacing of tasks, keeping everything moving forward.

Pacing takes practice, but here are some principles you can use to control the pace of your journey toward Opening Night:

• **The bigger the potential conflict, the more time you need to allow your Director to vision cast.** More on this later.

• **The larger your church, the more time you need to budget for promotion.** There's a lot going on inside your church that is clamoring for your people's attention. The bigger your congregation, the more time it's going to take your team's Opening Night concept to rise to the top of anyone's priority list.

• **Your team members have lives, children, spouses, jobs, yards, and bills.** You might be a full-time children's director, but chances are the majority of your team members are volunteers. Respect their lives and schedules.

> The majority of your team members are volunteers. Respect their lives and schedules.

• **You also have a life—whether you remember it or not.** You're in a race, but it's a marathon—not a sprint. Stay balanced.

• **You're probably managing more than one Opening Night concept.** Test your calendar against other projects on your horizon. If you dedicate 80 hours a week to this project for three weeks, what will happen to the project due next month?

• **The longer the journey to the Promised Land, the more "rest stops" you'll need to program for affirmation and midcourse corrections.** Remember, you die-hard Production Assistants: Your map is a tool to get you to the Promised Land. It's not a divinely inspired document that can never be tweaked. Plan for tweaking.

4. Convince Your Director and Leadership Team That Your Map Will Work

It's time to sell your road map to your team. You need to convince your Director on the merits of working the plan you've so carefully laid out. Team members must buy in that your map is trustworthy because they're going to have to take on tasks along the way.

Maps don't make journeys. People make journeys. It's the *people* you've got to convince, because otherwise all you've got is a nicely written plan that's going nowhere.

Let's imagine you've mapped out your Director's Opening Night concept from initial vision casting right down to the thank-you notes for helping clean up at the victory celebration. The map is complete, every task connected to a deadline and assigned to a champion. It's a perfect road map for change.

So what could go wrong?

It's quite possible that not everyone will *want* to change. Why? A big change can interrupt habits, challenge values, or strip players of their vested power.

Change can be the straw that breaks the camel's back. Change can be a headache if volunteers are having a difficult time in their marriages or managing a troubled teen.

Some personalities are just better at adjusting to change than others. It's quite possible that your team's Opening Night concept will be met with stiff resistance.

One person's Promised Land is another person's New Jersey. OK, *Siberia*.

Remember Moses leading God's people from slavery in the last chapter? The whole issue of change nearly caused God's people to toss out the road map and return to Egypt. People grumbled at their change in lifestyle and diet to the point that slavery and onions began to look good to them.

I used to love playing a board game called Risk. The point of the game is to deploy faceless armies over a world map, beating down enemies and obstacles until you dominate the board. Once upon a time, that's how I managed change.

That is, until I prayed the "10-year" prayer.

the 10-year prayer

I was in my early twenties, fresh out of college and working at a children's mental health residential treatment facility. It was my first real job. The pay stunk and the work was hard—*really* hard.

When it came time for my first performance evaluation, I was shocked. I was offered a 3 percent raise. I protested: I was one of the hardest workers in the agency. When I asked what was up, I discovered that the union didn't negotiate merit raises.

Being equal parts ignorant and arrogant, I decided the union had to go. (Looking for a new job honestly never entered my mind.) After a little research I learned how to file a petition to ask for my co-workers to vote on whether the union should be decertified.

Within a few weeks I'd collected the required signatures and filed the petition with the National Labor Relations Board. Life was good.

That is, until I was notified that I had made a *huge* mistake. I forgot to have my co-workers date their signatures. That seemingly small mistake—which would have been avoided if I had paid for a lawyer to help me—led to an eight-month court battle over the legitimacy of the petitions.

Those eight months were an emotional battle. Lots of tension flew around the agency. At first the union tried to recruit me as their new steward. When that didn't work, I started receiving legal notices from their Philadelphia lawyers. I scanned the letters to make sure I wasn't being sued for money or being required to appear in any courtroom.

Then I tossed the letters in the trash.

> **I had taken my best energy and spent it on something that wasn't God's kingdom.**

The NLRB ruled the employees could vote to decertify the union. The day of the vote came. I swallowed the tension in the air and became sick to my stomach. The anticipation was unbearable. At the end of the day they tallied up the votes.

We won by one vote. The union was decertified.

I expected to be elated. The eight-month conflict had ended. I learned how to endure under immense pressure. But there was no celebration, no fireworks. Nothing.

In fact, the one thing that all my co-workers seemed to agree on was that I was the lightning rod and that it wasn't safe to be seen with me, no matter how they voted.

It was the one of the loneliest days of my life. Then it hit me—I invested nearly a year of my life fighting over a paycheck. All those self-righteous arguments about fair pay, capitalism, and the American Way all evaporated. I had taken my best energy and spent it on something that wasn't God's kingdom.

I prayed, asking God to allow me to use the lessons I learned in this conflict to serve the church.

God answered that prayer for 10 straight years. The church that I grew up in began to sharply decline in numbers. The pastor was bi-vocational, and allegations about his temperament and leadership abilities began to surface in both arenas of his life.

The congregation appointed me to a small team of leaders to sort out the conflict and to deal with the allegations against the pastor. Truth be told, everyone did a tremendously horrid job. The pastor became defensive and maneuvered to hold onto his pulpit. My team was good-intentioned but absolutely ill-equipped to manage the conflict.

I'm convinced that some of the moves our team made only contributed to the pastor's defensive behavior. Our poor execution of conflict resolution and the presence of a few loose cannons on the team gave the pastor little reason to trust us.

The congregation? Well, they either fled, bled, or gossiped.

It wasn't pretty. After a few years of increasing strain, the pastor preached a fiery sermon denouncing every member of the team by name and stormed out the side door.

He threw bombs into the crowd and left us holding the body bags.

It became my job to provide the weekly preaching and lead the team to hire the next pastor. In short, my role became to help the church members manage change, and that's what I did for the next few years.

Shortly after the next senior pastor was hired, I moved to my fiancé's church, Grace Church. Within a year, I became the children's pastor. What I didn't realize was that Grace was also embroiled in massive conflict. It was transitioning from a small church to a regional church. Changes were being made in worship style and polity. The place was embroiled in the flames of controversy.

Speaking of flames, one of the staff member's children intentionally burnt the elementary children's wing to the ground.

Miraculously, with the help of a skilled conflict resolution specialist, the church and staff stayed together. Today, Grace is a thriving, healthy church. We've purchased 31 acres, and we're hip deep in the process of moving.

My connection to all that conflict was the result of my 10-year prayer.

The point of this story: I've learned through pain, sleepless nights, and many tears that leading people and their emotions through a change process is absolutely different than moving armies on a Risk board.

As Production Assistant, you have two responsibilities to the team…

- map the change process efficiently, and
- map the change process harmoniously.

The team members, parents, and children you work with aren't pawns. Furthermore, the shortest distance between where you are today and the Promised Land isn't always a straight line: Sometimes it's a route that avoids unnecessary casualties.

Here are some tips for building a road map if you need to navigate your team through a minefield of conflict…

- Schedule opportunities for the Director(s) on your team to share the vision often—both in large and small group settings.

Here are some tips for building a road map if you need to navigate your team through a minefield of conflict…

- Schedule opportunities for the Drama Coach(es) on your team to train people with the necessary values that are needed to appreciate the change as a positive thing.

- Schedule forums for upset, unsettled, and confused people to ask questions and challenge the plan. Conflict situations breed lots of talk. You can either program healthy opportunities for people to process their emotions, or you doom those people to become gossips.

- During times of conflict, schedule check points where the team can decide if the congregation can handle the pace of change. It's irresponsible to rush people through a change. However, it's equally irresponsible to stop marching to the Promised Land because you have opposition.

Disclaimer: Scheduling for conflict won't make all your opposition evaporate. That's just wishful thinking. However, you *can* reduce the frustration and "body count" by giving your volunteers and congregation time to manage their emotions in a Christlike manner.

Will that strategy require you to take longer getting to the Promised

Land? Yes…but it dramatically increases the chances of your getting everyone else there, too.

a production assistant's prayer

Dear God,
Thank you for how you wired me to lead. In the great drama of re-demption, you've asked me to create maps that will guide our children's ministry to our Promised Land. Help me choose the right path for our team. When the team deviates from the plan, give me flexibility and wis-dom to help keep us on course.

Help me build maps that help us bring as many people along with us as possible on the journey. By your grace, I will serve you by bringing both harmony and efficiency to our team's journey into the future.

In Jesus' name, amen.

for reflection and discussion

1. Is your ministry currently benefiting from the leadership gifts of a skilled Production Assistant?

If so, how is your ministry benefiting?

If not, brainstorm who in your congregation could help fill this void. Write their names here:

_____

_____

_____

_____

_____

2. Think about an intense conflict that you've gone through. How much of that conflict was created by people's reaction to change?

3. Whether or not you're a natural Production Assistant, you can in-corporate Production Assistant skills into your leadership portfolio.

Write down a few skills from this chapter that you'd like to add to your leadership repertoire.

a)_____

_____

b)_____

_____

c)_____

_____

Endnote

1. Walter C. Kaiser Jr., *A History of Israel* (Nashville, TN: Broadman and Holman Publishers, 1998), 276.

CHAPTER (5)

the **stage manager**

As Debbie hustled to get ready for rehearsal, *she marveled at what an impact Patricia had made on the chaos of the prior week.*

First, Patricia and Debbie had met with the choir director. They conceded that the choir should continue to use the sanctuary and offered to have the musical cast rehearse at another time. Together, Patricia, Debbie, and the choir director designed a rehearsal schedule that met everyone's needs.

Next, the team submitted a budget to the trustees. Debbie apologized for impulsively launching the musical without going through channels. Patricia presented a fund-raising plan that would cover most of the expenses. The trustees softened and gave the musical their blessing.

Pastor Jack heard about the meeting and thanked Debbie for making things right. Jack promised to sit in the front row on open-ing night.

Patricia had created a "road map" that was advancing the team to success.

They'd turned a corner. Everything felt right.

At least until the rehearsal began.

That's when the wheels feel off. First, Tom brought snacks for the kids just as he'd promised. However, the snacks were dozens of gourmet cinnamon rolls he'd picked up at the mall—the most expensive snacks in town.

"Nothing is too good for the kids!" Tom grinned as he turned in his receipt for reimbursement.

Debbie flinched. There was no way she could give this receipt to the trustees. Besides, she suddenly realized she had no clue how to go about being reimbursed for anything. Dollar signs popped into her head as she looked ahead to T-shirts, props, and costumes that would need to be purchased.

Pushing those thoughts out of her head, she began the rehearsal. This was the "blocking" rehearsal, when she'd show children where they needed to be on the stage throughout the musical.

Debbie knew it would be a long process, but she assumed they'd at least get to the end of Act One.

Five minutes into the musical the blocking screeched to a halt. Scene One was set in a playground, and the kids were supposed to be sitting on park benches or passing balls to each other.

No benches were handy.

One of the volunteers, Sue, quickly improvised and rounded up a few piano benches from around the church. Within 10 minutes, things were moving again.

Debbie noticed Sue open a notebook and sketch a few notes.

Sue's note-taking didn't end there. During Scene Two, Sue made a note when there wasn't a Bible for Johnny to pick up, and another note when Johnny forgot to take the Bible offstage with him at the end of the scene.

It seemed that every five minutes progress halted as some detail was ironed out. Each time, Sue opened her notebook and jotted a note. Debbie grimaced. Another confrontation was coming.

Sure enough, after the parents scooped up their children and left, Sue made a beeline for Debbie. She opened her notebook. "Debbie, we need to talk."

Debbie was crestfallen—she had to face yet another critic. As Debbie mentally prepared her defense, Sue spoke: "I'd like to help. I'm kind of a freak for detail. During the rehearsal, I made a list of things that need to be done. There's just a lot of minutiae. I don't know how you can be expected to keep up with it.

"If you don't mind, I'd like to be your Stage Manager. I'll administer the small stuff so you can focus on Directing.

"You're doing a great job. I could never mobilize a team like you're doing. But I can serve the team by tying up all the loose ends before they become a problem. I sort of enjoy creating order and routine."

Debbie breathed a sigh of relief.

"That would be great. Hey, do you think you could help me come up with a way to handle the receipts and the financial side of the musical? It's just too big a job for me to do by myself..."

That night, Debbie pondered her team as she sipped a cup of tea. The whole musical was like going on a journey. She pointed out the destination. Patricia was the navigator, providing the maps. Sue was like the mom who wrote the packing lists so everyone remembered to take along all the stuff that was needed.

Debbie allowed herself a brief smile. "I think we are going to get there after all."

profile of a stage manager

The Stage Manager has an eye for details. In the theater world, stage managers lead by seeing all of the loose ends that need to be tied up in order for the play to be successfully produced.

There are props to purchase. It's not enough for the script to call for a dictionary to be sitting on the mantle in Scene One. Someone has to

learning the parts If you think you might be a Stage Manager, reread the "Profile of a Stage Manager" again, this time with a highlighter pen in hand. The profile is a composite description of Stage Managers in general, but you know yourself best.

Customize the profile to fit yourself. Highlight sentences that your spouse or friends would point to and say, "Yup—that's you!" Place a star next to sentences that don't describe you at all.

If you know you *aren't* a Stage Manager, decide if you have a Stage Manager in your life. Does this description remind you of anyone in your church or children's ministry? Jot down the names of those people below.

_____

_____

_____

_____

notice that detail, purchase the dictionary, and place it on the mantle.

Oh—and someone needs to make sure there's a mantle on which to set the dictionary.

In a children's ministry setting, the Stage Manager has the ability to see the details that everyone else seems to overlook or forget. The Stage Manager leads by taking care of all the pesky details. Details which, if they aren't tended to, could stop a project cold.

Pesky details like…

• making sure the security bracelets are ordered for the Sunday school department.

• seeing that the nursery has a health policy and that someone is routinely sanitizing the toys.

• double-checking to guarantee that contracts were signed with the summer camp.

• making sure that snacks and drinks are purchased and in the supply closet.

A vibrant children's ministry has a lot of balls in the air at any given moment. A Stage Manager leads by keeping those balls from hitting the ground.

Stage Managers are frequently seen carrying clipboards or PDAs, sizing up classrooms, and making to-do lists. Stage Managers have an eye for seeing what systems need to be put in place and what has to happen for the ministry to operate efficiently.

They often measure how successful a day was by how many tasks are checked off the list.

Seasoned Stage Managers have a sort of organizational X-ray vision; they can analyze their to-do lists and envision how routines can be put in place that will fix problems once and for all. That occasional problem of nursery volunteers forgetting to take the dirty diapers out to the trash bin? A Stage Manager will soon have a Dirty Diaper Management page added to the Nursery Department Policy Book, and every volunteer will be trained on how to find the trash bin.

Look at a Stage Manager's computer: There's a reminder in the Stage Manager's personal organizing software that prompts the purchase of curriculum and security supplies four times a year...and in time to qualify for the discount.

Walk into a Stage Manager's supply closet, and you'll see neat rows of plastic tubs, all perfectly labeled.

A Stage Manager vigilantly looks for new ways to improve the efficiency of the children's ministry.

A Stage Manager vigilantly looks for new ways to improve the efficiency of the children's ministry. When a Stage Manager finds a way to create even *more* order in that already immaculate supply closet, it makes the Stage Manager's day.

Stage Managers take pleasure in knowing they helped create an orderly environment in which people can serve. Since Stage Managers often feel most secure when they operate within clearly defined boundaries and expectations, they're motivated to create that sense of security for their teammates.

Stage Managers dislike working in unstructured environments. It's unnerving to them. That's why they work so hard to keep the balls from dropping. And that's why Stage Managers create policies and systems—to help their team members serve in an anxiety-free environment.

Which is wonderful...unless someone doesn't want to live in a world defined by systems and policies.

Stage Managers have difficulty understanding team members who ignore details and protocol. They often see these free spirits as mavericks and troublemakers. Stage Managers face the challenge of "selling" the value of protocols to their more adventurous teammates.

Stage Managers must be careful to not generate so many policies and procedures that their team members feel suffocated by red tape. A Stage Manager looks at a policy and sees a helpful fence. However, teammates might look at the same policy and see prison bars.

Who is right? Well, that's a matter of perception that can only be determined by the team—and hammered out during dialogue.

A Stage Manager looks at a policy and sees a helpful fence.

Stage Managers bless the church—and your ministry—by providing the star leadership of tending the Toolbox and providing Muscle. Their keen eye for details allows leaders who have a more global eye to keep focused on the big picture.

You remember that old adage: "You can't see the forest for the trees." Directors and Production Assistants usually see the forest. Stage Managers tend to have an easier time seeing the trees.

That's a good thing, because a forest is built tree by tree. Someone needs to have an eye for detail and nurture each and every tree. Stage Managers are the foresters of the church. As they tend to each tree, they're helping build a forest.

Stage Managers are also capable Toolbox managers. They're ideal people to think through what needs to be in your ministry's policy book. As they hear questions asked by volunteers, Stage Managers see what needs to be in the ministry's policy book.

Stage Managers listen for questions like these:

• "How do I go about getting reimbursed for money I spend on a lesson?"

• "How often am I expected to straighten up my classroom?"

• "Am I allowed to give a child a painkiller when he or she has a headache?"

When questions like these reach the ears of a Stage Manager, you can bet there will be three new policies in the next edition of the policy book.

The result is that when volunteers have a pressing question and need information quickly, the Stage Manager has often already placed that information in the children's ministry's toolbox.

Bible case study of a stage manager: JOSEPH

Joseph (the Joseph of many-colored-coat fame) is a fantastic example of a biblical Stage Manager.

Throughout Genesis' account of Joseph's life, we see Joseph's concern for order. In fact, in the very first verse that Joseph is mentioned in Scripture, we see him giving a bad report on his brothers for the way they mismanaged their father's flocks (Genesis 37:2).

Joseph's tense relationship with his older brothers led to the brothers selling Joseph into slavery in Egypt. Joseph found himself a slave in the house of Potiphar, the captain of Pharaoh's guard (Genesis 39:1). Whatever responsibilities Pharaoh assigned Joseph, Joseph successfully accomplished. Potiphar promoted Joseph to the Egyptian rank of "lord," which is the equivalent of the Hebrew title "administrator."[1]

Joseph led through administration. He brought order and organization to every aspect of Potiphar's household—the finances, the work force—every aspect of Potiphar's world was being effectively administered.

Potiphar prospered under the God-honoring leadership of a Stage Manager. Genesis 39:5 states that God's blessing was on every aspect of Potiphar's estate.

Later, Joseph's wrongful imprisonment had no impact on his high character and leadership voice. Even in those chaotic times, Joseph used his God-given ability to create order. The prison warden was so moved by Joseph that he made Joseph the administrator of the entire prison.

The warden was able to stop paying attention to the day-to-day operations due to Joseph's command of the situation (Genesis 39:20-23).

Then Joseph's fortune changed radically. His ability to interpret dreams was reported to the Pharaoh, who charged Joseph with interpreting a dream. That dream had huge implications: After seven years of good harvests, a famine would ravage Egypt for seven years.

Joseph not only interpreted the dream, but he immediately proposed a system to create a national grain reserve. Joseph recommended a national system of administrators who would make sure that farmers gave a fifth of their grain to the government for seven years. Those reserves would feed Egypt during the famine.

The Pharaoh was so impressed that he fired Joseph as a consultant and hired him to be the administrator over the entire nation of Egypt.

Imagine that! Joseph was only 30 years old, and he was charged with rescuing Egypt by implementing a system of order. Joseph's efforts paid off.

Early in the process, Joseph carefully counted how much grain was collected. However, eventually so much grain was collected that it was impossible to count (Genesis 41:49).

When the famine struck, the nation was prepared. So prepared that Joseph was able to sell surplus grain to other countries blighted by the famine.

Ultimately, the grain surplus that Joseph created caught the attention of his family (Genesis 42:1-2) and drew them to Egypt.

for discussion and reflection

1. Joseph brought order to four radically different organizations—the sheep industry, a personal estate, a state prison, and then a world superpower. Why do you think Joseph was able to take on the administrative needs of four increasingly complex organizations?

2. If Joseph joined your team, what changes would he initiate in your children's ministry?

Think about that—by exercising his Stage Managing leadership style, Joseph saved his family. Jacob and his sons were in real danger of dying of starvation.

It wasn't a warrior, a visionary leader, or a prophet who saved Egypt and countless families and tribes who lived beyond Egypt's borders. It was a Stage Manager. If there were clipboards in those days, Joseph would have been carrying one instead of a sword.

God can use any style of leader to accomplish his will.

contemporary case study: jeanette chase

Jeanette Chase is the director of U18 Ministries at Crossroads Church in Mansfield, Ohio. Jeanette leads through a unique and powerful blend of leadership voices. She's both a Director and a Stage Manager. Like her biblical counterpart, Joseph, Jeanette is able to see visions and create systems that allow the vision to come to pass.

Before joining the staff at Crossroads as the Children's Ministry Director, Jeanette served as an executive secretary at The Disney Company. According to Jeanette, this is where she mastered the Stage Manager skill set. It was a fast-paced environment that required administrative excellence. She learned how to organize in such a way that she was able to keep all vital information at her fingertips.

As Crossroads' first paid children's ministry staff member, Jeanette's skills served her well. Jeanette used her visionary skills to pioneer a new model of children's ministry that resonated with the Big Church culture. (See Chapter 3 for some practical how-to's if you need to do the same thing.)

However, because everything Jeanette did was new to the volunteer base, she also quickly built systems that provided her volunteers with a sense of security.

After installing a "large group/small group" model for Sunday mornings, she quickly wrote job descriptions that clearly let team members know what was expected of them.

Next, Jeanette organized teams to write policies and procedures covering safety, screening, and discipline. Jeanette stresses the value of crafting the procedures in a *team* environment.

"It creates buy-in. I'm not forcing rules onto the team. My job is to be the visionary, to do the research. I need to provide my teams with the information needed to make them *want* to have good policies. For example, when we created the volunteer screening policies, I researched national statistics on churches and child abuse," says Jeanette.

Jeanette organized her teams' work into a volunteer handbook. "The handbook provides order for the volunteers—they never have to guess what's expected of them."

Next, Jeanette created a vision-supporting system to make the teaching team's job more orderly. Twice a month, "e-teams" (the "e" is for *excellence*) come to the church to organize all of the crafts and snacks for teachers. "The volunteers love it," reports Jeanette. "The extra organization allows them to focus on their primary task—teaching God's word effectively."

> Jeanette stresses the value of crafting the procedures in a *team* environment.

Jeanette brought vision to her ministry. But unlike many Directors, she also brought order. According to Jeanette, everyone benefits from a well-ordered ministry...

• **Volunteers:** "Volunteers need to work in an organized setting. You need to remove the frustrations that can distract them from focusing on the big picture"

• **Parents:** "I share my volunteer handbook with any parent who asks to see it. You can't overcommunicate with parents. When a parent sees that you've thought through your ministry and are organized, that parent will give you his or her trust."

• **Kids:** "Children benefit from having a relaxed teacher. When a teacher walks into an organized classroom and is ready to relax and enjoy the children as they come in, it makes for a nicer classroom. Kids notice that. It makes the whole learning experience beneficial for them."

Like Joseph, Jeanette's Stage Manager skills created opportunities for professional advancement. She was recently promoted from Director of Children's Ministries to Director of U18. In her new position, she now supervises youth, children, and college ministries. The scope of her ministry has grown, in a large part, because she is an effective Stage Manager.

how to be a stage manager— whether you are one or not

Whether you're a *natural* Stage Manager looking to sharpen your skills or someone who just needs to *behave* like a Stage Manager, here's your step-by-step guide to success.

Stage Managers: This section is chock-full of lists—right up your alley. Get ready to sharpen your administrative skills.

Not a natural Stage Manager? Neither am I. Don't get me wrong. I'm an Outlook and PDA junkie. But when push comes to shove and the pace of life gets *really* hairy, my global side wins out. I become more "big picture" oriented and have a hard time focusing on the details.

That's when I'm glad I acted like a Stage Manager during the calm times and built my task lists then. I'll pretend to be a Stage Manager, although it's not really "me." Call it hypocrisy if you want. I call it "staying employed."

Let me tell you a story…

A long time ago, before I was married and had three kids, I had something very special—free time. I used some of that free time to try my hand at acting at a local community theater.

In a murder mystery, I played the part of a jealous husband. My character was one of the "red herrings," created to draw attention away from the real killer. After two months of playing the inanely jealous spouse, an unsettling thing happened.

After one rehearsal, the boyfriend of the actress who was cast as my wife showed up on the set. Now that's a natural and good thing. Except I felt a pang of possessiveness and jealousy. It was a fleeting emotion, and, to be truthful, it creeped me out.

The experience stuck with me because it reminds me of a leadership truth: I can be and think like any style of leadership I wish, if I am willing to invest enough energy. To some extent, I'll become the person I pretend to be.

So can you.

So whether you were born a Stage Manager or you're going to fake your way into being one, let's tackle this style.

There are two levels of Stage Management:

Level One: "See-Capture-Do"

Level Two: Systems Builder

level one: "see-capture-do"

The process is remarkably straightforward: To be an effective Stage Manager you first need to observe what needs to be accomplished, capture that task on your to-do list, and then get the job done.

It *sounds* simple, but this simple process is the "make or break" test for many leaders. Do you remember the old picture of the three monkeys who "see no evil, speak no evil, hear no evil"?

Many would-be leaders either "see no task," "remember no task," or "do no task." If you are weak at any one of these three steps, you're going to fail to execute a task that needs to be accomplished for your team to reach the Promised Land.

• See

Stage Managers have an uncanny ability to look at a Promised Land concept and instantly see the jobs that need to be done. Directors see the Promised Land. Production Assistants see the maps. Stage Managers see lists.

Drop a Stage Manager into a classroom, and he or she will instantly generate a list of what toys need to be cleaned, what shelves require organizing, and what forms should be placed in the teacher mailboxes.

A Stage Manager can look at a Production Assistant's calendar and immediately identify what tasks need to be accomplished to keep progress moving forward.

Not a Stage Manager by trade? Here are some tips to improve your powers of observation.

- Ask volunteers to tell you what frustrates them as teachers.
- Create work-request forms so volunteers can tell you what needs to be fixed in your classrooms.
- Imagine that you have to explain to a brand-new volunteer what it takes to pull off an event. Write down everything that needs to happen in order for the event to work.

- Make sure you aren't wearing any blinders. Some would-be leaders don't *want* to see the needs around them. Some of those blinders include a belief that a task isn't your job…or that you don't have time…or that the task is just too big to tackle.

If you wear one or more set of blinders long enough, you can get to the point where you honestly aren't aware of the needs around you. That's the wrong place for a leader to be.

• Capture

Once you've seen the job, you need to *remember* it. I can't tell you how many times I've left my office to get a task done, been stopped by three people along the way, and then paused as I realized that I couldn't remember what in the world I left the office for. I'm not the only one, right?

I've also talked with a volunteer on Sunday about a situation that arose in a classroom, promising to follow up on Tuesday. Unfortunately, I completely forgot about the situation by Sunday dinner.

I just don't have a mind built to hold details.

In my ministry I wasn't a total organizational slob, but I knew I was dropping too many details. Over the years a wonderful wife, three kids, and a dog have joined me on my life's journey— each one demanding some of my time, each one bringing their own to-do lists for me. Things were getting more complex, and I knew I had to take some drastic measures.

So I became a cyborg, part man and part machine.

Do you remember that old action show that was on TV in the '70s, *The Six Million Dollar Man*? (For the annoyingly young readers, the show was about an astronaut who survived a terrible wreck. Scientists saved his life with bionic parts that gave him superhuman strength.)

> **Some would-be leaders don't *want* to see the needs around them.**

What happened to me isn't that dramatic. Sorry. I just bought a handheld PDA. The PDA allows me to create to-do lists and to capture names, phone numbers, and dates wherever I am, right on the spot. I can connect the PDA to my computer and synchronize the information to my Outlook program. It's far more efficient than the bulk paper system I was using.

It really doesn't matter if you use a PDA, a paper day-planner system, or sidewalk chalk and the church parking lot: The point is, *write everything down*. Immediately.

Next to my PDA, my next favorite organizational tool is a giant, laminated, "year-at-a-glance" calendar. I put everything on it—every major event on the church calendar goes there.

If your church has a calendar and event database, learn how to use it. Get the secretary or resident computer geek to show you the ropes. If you are ever going to be an expert Stage Manager, you need to be a master at "capturing it."

If your church has a calendar and event database, learn how to use it.

• Do

After you've observed the problem and recorded it on your to-do list, now it's time to get it done. Don't put things off, don't procrastinate, just do it.

At the beginning of each week, make a list of what you need to accomplish. Next, rank the items in order of importance. What needs to be done *now*? What tasks are mission critical, and what can wait?

What tasks are most closely connected to who God called you to be? What needs to be done to take care of your family?

Only you can determine the criteria that you will use to rank your priorities. I could rank your list, but it would reflect *my* agenda.

Once you've ranked your list, it's game time! Start with the most important things on your list and start getting things done. As you move through your week, you'll be picking up new to-do's. You might need to reprioritize your list if new tasks become urgent.

Level One Stage Managers get more things accomplished than most people. However, there's a *higher* level of efficiency to be attained if you want to be a world-class Stage Manager.

Level One Stage Managers operate like simple microorganisms. There's a stimulus—something to be done—and the Stage Manager responds. He or she writes it down and does it. Task after task, problem after problem.

In Level One, you are always *reacting* to needs as they surface. What if you could anticipate tasks *before* they happened? What if you could script the responses of every volunteer who encountered a particular task so the volunteer took care of the need? If you could provide training and information that took care of issues before those issues became problems?

Level Two Stage Managers can do just that.

level two: systems builder

If Level One Stage Managers are like single-celled organisms that react to their environment, Level Two Stage Managers are like larger, complex animals—people, for instance. They do more than just react to the environment…they impact it proactively.

Think about all of the body systems God built into us humans—muscular, nervous, lymphatic, circulatory, and digestive, just to name a few.

Each system is designed to handle predictable, routine tasks such as breathing, pumping blood, or converting food into fuel, vitamins, and minerals. To take the biology lesson just a bit further, allow me to point out that the human body has two types of systems: somatic and autonomic.

Somatic, or voluntary systems, take thought. In order to move your arm to pick up a hamburger, you need to first "will" it to happen. The act of moving your jaw to eat the burger is also a somatic response.

Autonomic, or involuntary, systems function inside your body without you having to put any thought into them. You don't need to remember to breathe or think about making your heart pump blood. Your glands don't need a memo to secrete hormones.

If you had to consciously think about these behaviors, you'd never get much else done.

"See-Capture-Do" activities are all somatic responses. They are as necessary as eating. However, there's a problem. Each one requires thought and mental energy. The more mental energy your volunteers have to spend on things like locating supplies or knowing a safe way to respond to a child's nosebleed, the less energy they have to spend on making your Opening Night picture become a reality.

An interview by Dave Spadaro with Philadelphia Eagles head coach, Andy Reid, captures this truth:

Q: Why is there generally such a significant improvement [by individual players] from year one to year two in the NFL?

Reid: "I think it's a matter of walking in the same footsteps you walked the first time. Any time you go over uncovered ground or territory, it's a little bit harder the first time you do it. You learn so much. You learn the routine of the 'house.' You learn about offense and defense and special teams at this level. It's a whole new world. You've got to get used to your coach; you've got to get used to the speed of the game. You learn things like, 'How do I get to the stadium? Where do I park?' All of those simple, little things you need to learn. The list goes on and on. In your second year, you just do those things. They are already part of your routine. You don't have to think about them. You can just do your job."[2]

> **"I think it's a matter of walking in the same footsteps you walked the first time."**

Level Two Managers serve their teams by building routines that allow new team members to quickly learn the ropes so team members can focus on what matters most.

Here's a sample of a few children's ministry functions that should be a part of your children's ministry's autonomic systems:
- financial reimbursement
- managing budget/receipts
- health policies
- safety
- evacuation/fire drill procedures
- universal precautions
- ordering supplies and curriculum

policies and procedures

Once you know what task you want to move from your children's ministry's somatic systems to the ministry's autonomic systems, it's time to create policies and procedures. Depending on your background, the phrase "policies and procedures" can make your eyes glaze over or prompt nightmares about smothering under a landslide of bureaucracy.

It doesn't have to be that way. Honestly. Let's look at what it takes to build good policies and procedures, and then we'll look at how to keep them from ruling your ministry.

• Policies

According to Webster's Dictionary, the word *policy* comes from the middle English word, *policie,* meaning citizenship. So it would make sense that policies need to somehow help people who follow them be better citizens of a society or an organization. Your policies need to somehow promote the greater good of your children's ministry.

You can convince team members that policies matter by appealing to what your team already values. For example, a policy explaining classroom security could appeal to the fact that God loves children and that you have been called to be stewards of those kids, to make sure they're safe. You could also explain that obeying the security policies will allow visiting parents to feel secure dropping off their children, allowing the parents to participate in your worship service and hear the gospel without distraction.

Here's a test: If you're writing a policy or procedure and you're unable to make a strong connection between the system and greater good of your children's ministry, stop. Rip up the paper and throw it away. You need that document like you need another hole in the head. Something else is going on inside you—perhaps you're having some control issues?

Whatever it is, take a deep breath and let it go. Your team will thank you.

• Procedures

A procedure is a simple list of behaviors that need to occur whenever a specified situation arises. Using our classroom security example, a simple procedure to describe what needs to happen when visiting parents bring a preschool child to a classroom might be...

1. Warmly welcome the child to the classroom. Introduce yourself to the parents and child.

2. Ask the parents to register their child using the proper sign-in sheet. Your form should capture information such as child's name, age, special needs, and where the parents will be during the worship service.

3. Explain the security wristband system to both the child and the parents. Place the band securely around the child's ankle or wrist, and give the matching number end to the parent.

4. Introduce the visiting child to your teaching partner and other children.

5. Ask the parents if they have any questions about your children's ministry or the church.

6. Explain how you'll enter the child's wristband number into the silent pager system so parents can be notified if their child becomes upset and the parents are needed.

> **If you can't read [your procedure] in one minute, it's too long.**

Here are some tips for writing good procedures:

Use simple language. Your volunteers are looking for a quick "how to." They aren't picking up your policy manual for a good read.

Use action language. A procedure is a guideline for action, so use action verbs like *say*, *write*, *record*, or *bandage*. Present tense action verbs let the volunteers know what's expected of them.

Be brief. Read your procedure aloud. If you can't read it in one minute, it's too long. Use short, clear sentences.

Use new eyes. Don't assume that the reader knows *anything* about the task at hand. Write it like the person reading it has never spent a day in your ministry. Could a stranger read your procedure and feel confident that he or she could do the job correctly?

Double-check. Before publishing a new policy or procedure, have another person read it over. This second set of eyes will help you see any gaps in logic.

Consult history. Before you roll out an old policy, know what's already on the books. Are there conflicting policies and procedures in a file cabinet that you don't know about?

• Will the policy or procedure grow with you?

How often do you *really* want to have to write these things? Ask yourself: If God blesses your church and children's ministry and it doubles or triples in size, will the system still work?

• Borrow from your neighbor

…with their blessing, of course. Children's ministries all over the country have similar policy needs. Many children's ministries publish their handbooks on the Internet.

You can find these manuals by using an Internet browser (www .google.com is one) and typing "children's ministry policy manual" in the search engine. In seconds, you'll have access to policy manuals from other children's ministries.

If you aren't tech savvy, call a few of the larger churches in town and ask them for a copy of their children's ministry handbooks. Or get a membership to Group Publishing's Church Volunteer Central (call 1-800-761-2095 or visit www.group.com) and take a look at the hundreds of job descriptions, policies, and procedures they've assembled for your review.

My point: You can save a lot of time and energy by not reinventing the wheel.

• Burn a reflex

You've written a concise and clear policy. Great. But your work has just begun. The goal is to get your team members to internalize the policies and procedures to the point where they understand it and do it without having to think about it. Remember that you're creating an *autonomic* system.

Here's another way to look at it: You're trying to move your policies and procedures from your children's ministry's mind memory into it's muscle memory. In tae kwon do, every time Master Mancino taught me a new kick or combination strike, I'd have to think about every part of the kick. My movement was tentative because of all the energy it took me to focus on the mechanics of the kick and balance.

The only way to get past it was through repetition. Mancino would make us practice the new skill repeatedly, on each side of the body, until it became second nature.

You haven't created an autonomic system until the desired behavior is second nature for your team. You need to burn the desired behavior into your team's muscle memory.

Here are some tips on moving from a mere paper policy to corporate muscle memory:

• Train your team
If Stage Manager isn't a prominent part of your leadership voice, then tap a capable teammate. Train your team not only about the "what" but the "why" of policies and procedures.

> Train your team not only about the "what" but the "why" of policies and procedures.

• Appeal to your core values
Internalizing a new policy takes a lot of work for your team. Remind your team that this new way of doing business connects with the highest goals of your team.

• Expect some resistance
Don't expect immediate buy-in from everyone. Hold your ground, but politely listen and try to discover the source of any resistance.

• Inspect!
Very few volunteers will take the time and effort to convert policy into habit unless they know that you care enough to check for follow through. What gets measured is what gets done, so inspect, inspect, inspect.

• Evaluate and simplify
Revisit your policies and procedures after nine to 12 months to see if

they're achieving the desired results. See if there's anything cumbersome you can simplify.

Order is good. However, the fine line between a suffocating bureaucracy and a life-giving organization is made of red tape. Keep your team on the right side of that line.

When you stay on the correct side of the line, you're leading your team. You're even reflecting an attribute of God's nature. Scripture reminds us "God is not a God of disorder but of peace."

As you lead with the Stage Manager voice, you're breathing God's order into your situation. Your team's journey to Opening Night can be characterized by chaos or it can be characterized by efficiency. Your influence brings harmony to the team and reduces frustration. The power of a God-honoring Stage Manager is immense and incalculable.

a stage manager's prayer

Dear God,

I thank you for wiring me the way you did. I pray that you will help me lead in a way that brings creation out of chaos. Help me create systems and calm that help my team serve you better. Protect me from making order the main thing, though. I understand that this journey can be messy and that it's full of surprises. I pray for flexibility and the ability to convince my team of the benefits of organization.

May I lead well for your name's sake.

Amen.

for reflection and discussion

1. Have you seen the positive influence of a powerful Stage Manager in your ministry? List those benefits on page 104. Also, take a minute and write that Stage Manager a thank-you note as a way of showing the person your appreciation.

2. When you think of policies and procedures, what sort of emotions

come to mind? Are those attitudes helping or hindering your ability to embrace the systems in your children's ministry?

3. Do you see any policies in your children's ministry that can be simplified? Ask yourself: If we stopped adhering to a certain policy, what could happen?

4. Is there anyone on your team whose organizational gifts aren't being utilized? Make an appointment to meet with that person and share your vision of a more organized ministry.

Endnotes

1. Walter C. Kaiser Jr., *A History of Israel* (Nashville, TN: Broadman and Holman Publishers,1998), 27.

2. http://philadelphiaeagles.com/homeNewsDetail.jsp?id=11351(Used with permission.)

CHAPTER 6

the **drama coach**

Flanked by Patricia and Sue, Debbie's *confidence was growing.*

Patricia made sure the team kept pace with the schedule she'd mapped out, and that the processes they'd put in place were met. Sue was an administrative marvel—she had a knack for seeing problems even before they happened.

Debbie finally could focus on what was happening on stage. When she did, she wasn't pleased with what she saw. The children just weren't…well…very good. Most children weren't even speaking loudly enough so people in the front row could hear them.

Little Robbie constantly fidgeted and was distracting everyone.

Debbie made a note of it on her clipboard, though she had no idea how she'd get Robbie to stop shifting from foot to foot and pulling at his clothes.

Debbie saw that the kids were standing in clumps, muttering and racing through their lines. Some of the children kept turning their backs to the audience.

Debbie wasn't the only one who noticed the problem. Mrs. Jones had enrolled Emily in Community Theater so long that Emily had practically grown up on stage, and Emily did deliver her lines with poise.

Unfortunately, off stage, Emily tore into her fellow cast members for their clumsy performances.

Visions of her niece's musical flashed back into Debbie's head. Those kids were able to pull it off, so why not her kids? What was she doing wrong?

Debbie explained the problems to the kids, but her cajoling and begging made no difference. Her kids just did not have it.

The next evening, Debbie shared her frustrations with her small group. Dan listened with interest. "See me after the Bible study," he said. "I think I can help."

Debbie didn't pay much attention to the lesson that night. The promise of a solution intrigued her. Within a minute of the "amen," Debbie cornered Dan by the snacks.

"So you think you have the cure for bad acting?" she asked.

Dan laughed. "Yeah, well at least a partial cure. Look, Debbie, these kids are green. They've never tried this before so of course they stink. What else would you expect? These kids need to learn the basic skills of acting.

"I'm no Harrison Ford, but I've done a few shows at community theaters. I know a thing or two about acting. I've also done some volunteer work with the youth theater. You mentioned Emily. I've worked with her quite a bit.

"If you want, I could teach your cast some basics. They won't be ready for Broadway anytime soon, but I can help them clean up some bad habits. Think about it."

"Sold. I don't need to think about anything," Debbie replied. "I don't know acting like you do. If you can make my other kids perform like Emily, then you're hired."

Debbie stuck out her hand. "The pay stinks and the hours are long. But you're my new Drama Coach."

A handshake, and the deal was done.

Debbie smiled. Vision, process leading, administration, and now coaching—every new addition to the team supplied the team with more leadership. Opening night was a little over a month away.

Debbie just knew the musical was going to be great.

profile of a drama coach

In the theater, a Drama Coach leads by teaching cast members the skills and competencies needed to become skilled actors.

Actors need to master dozens of skills, such as how to stand and move, how to project their voices, how to get into and stay in character, and how to play off other cast members. The Drama Coach is an experienced actor who knows how to pass his or her theater experience along to a new generation of actors.

In a ministry context, the Drama Coach leads by teaching team members the competencies, values, policies and procedures, and philosophies needed for the team to become master children's ministry volunteers.

A Drama Coach has "been there," knows what works, and knows how to help team members have the best chance of being successful in ministry.

A Drama Coach is conversant in both biblical knowledge and children's ministry know-how. Drama Coaches enjoy studying Scripture. It's inevitable: Even when Drama Coaches are reading the Bible for personal friendship with God, they're constantly thinking of ways they can teach their discoveries to others.

Beyond Scripture, Drama Coaches also are drawn to a broad field of literature in the business and education fields. They're on a constant quest to bring the best ideas into their children's ministries.

A good Drama Coach is able to present this wisdom in simple and memorable ways that motivate team members to change

learning the parts If you think you might be
a Drama Coach, reread the "Profile of a Drama Coach" again, this time
with a highlighter pen in hand. The profile is a composite description of
Drama Coaches in general, but you know yourself best.

Customize the profile to fit yourself. Highlight sentences that your
spouse or friends would point to and say, "No question about it—that
describes you!" Place a star next to sentences that don't describe you
at all.

If you know you *aren't* a Drama Coach, decide if you have a Drama
Coach in your life. Does this description remind you of anyone in your
church or children's ministry? Jot down the names of those people
below.

_____

_____

_____

_____

behavior. Drama Coaches measure their success not by lessons taught,
but by lessons learned. Drama Coaches want to see their team members
growing in spiritual maturity and children's ministry prowess.

World-class Drama Coaches feel most used by God when they are
training adults. They may have initially gotten into children's ministry
to work with children, but Drama Coaches discover the power of leading through training volunteers. The ministry potential of multiplying
their influence by investing in their peers is irresistible.

Drama Coaches constantly create opportunities to equip their team
members in either group or individual settings. Drama Coaches recognize the powerful dynamics that take place in large group teaching
experiences, but they also understand the impact one-on-one coaching has on developing new leaders and teachers.

Drama Coaches often have strong ideas about what skills and theories team members need to master in order to be effective children's ministers. To a Drama Coach, the value of mastering those skills and theories is crystal clear—and Drama Coaches are frustrated when team members don't see the value of attending training opportunities and developing those skills and theories.

Peers who see training as a waste of time or don't prioritize personal development are a puzzle to Drama Coaches. Drama Coaches can also be critical when they sit under less skilled trainers. Instead of gleaning the truths that might be learned, Drama Coaches often pass the time rewriting the lesson even as the trainer is still presenting it.

Drama Coaches need to be careful that they don't fall into the trap of pride or "information dumping." Ineffective Drama Coaches get caught up in the minutiae of teaching and focus on presenting interesting facts instead of presenting the raw materials of life-change.

In their brief but potent book, *The 1 Thing*™, Thom and Joani Schultz describe Drama Coaches who fall into this trap. "Information becomes something to possess. More is better. Its value becomes self-contained—knowledge for its own sake. Information can easily be more revered than understanding or application."[1]

On the other hand, a God-honoring Drama Coach serves his or her children's ministry by stocking the Toolbox with needed skills and tools. Drama Coaches help the whole team achieve a spectacular Opening Night vision by giving team members the tools needed to get there.

Bible case study of a drama coach: Jesus' critique of THE PHARISEES' discipleship process

Jesus' strategy of training his followers is well documented in the Gospels. Instead of just using lectures, Jesus used a discipleship model that was common during his time. Jesus gathered a small group of disciples, lived with them, and trained them in how to advance God's kingdom, even after he was gone.

Jesus' use of the discipleship model was hardly unique. Most teachers of the time used the discipleship model. A short list of other teachers implementing the approach includes John the Baptist, Plato, and the Pharisees.

However, because Jesus was fully God, we can assume a few things about his use of the Drama Coach leadership style...

• Jesus knew it was the most effective means possible to equip his followers for a lifetime of serving him. If there'd been a better approach, it's logical he'd have used it.

• Jesus was the perfect "Drama Coach." No teacher in the history of the world has taught better things or with more effective methods.

Keep those two truths in view as we look at Matthew 23. Jesus, Master Drama Coach, spends the entire chapter analyzing the way that the Pharisees had built their discipleship system.

Jesus reserved some of his harshest words to scold the way the Pharisees mangled the Drama Coach leadership style and built a dysfunctional learning culture. Let's look at Jesus' assessment of the Pharisaical education system to discover what went wrong...and to identify some positive principles for imitating Jesus' use of the Drama Coach style.

• The Pharisees didn't live what they taught (Matthew 23:1-4).

Jesus' opening salvo faults the Pharisees for burdening their disciples with the Mosaic Law, while at the same time ignoring those same rules. Verse 4 evokes images of Exodus: The disciples are enslaved by the demands of their teachers while the Pharisees stand idly watching.

Jesus' approach to living what he taught is summed up in James 3:1: Model what you expect from your learners. There is no "do as I say and not as I do" when you're coaching like Jesus coached.

• The Pharisees were in the coaching game for their own egos (Matthew 23:5-12).

Jesus scolded the Pharisees for being attention hounds. He ripped them for flashy teaching accessories (verse 5) and for using their position in society as a vehicle for inflating their own egos.

Jesus turned the Pharisees' approach on its head, to coaching by servant leadership. True leaders weren't in it for position and ego; they were there to serve and learn. In Matthew 23:8-12, Jesus tells how ego fits into leadership.

• The Pharisees' coaching didn't help their followers build a connection to God (Matthew 23:13, 15-24).

Here's the crux of Jesus' complaint against the Pharisees: Their coaching methods actually *prevented* their followers from becoming friends with God. Read verses 16-24 and compare the Pharisees' syllabus with the content of Matthew 5–7. Jesus taught his followers how to thrive in God's kingdom, while the Pharisees taught their followers how to wiggle out of verbal contracts and substitute right relationships for spiritual trivial pursuit.

The purpose of Jesus' coaching is clear: to bring about spiritual health.

• The Pharisees coached at a veneer-deep level (Matthew 23:25-28).

The Pharisees stopped coaching their followers when the followers achieved an outward, religious conformity. Since the unspoken goal of the Pharisees was social power, their coaching objectives centered on making the Pharisees look good as an organization. Jesus regarded their entire operation as a gift-wrapped garbage dump. Pharisees were ceremonial savants but relationally bankrupt; God was not a part of their emotional transactions.

Jesus coached with depth. He wasn't interested in making his ministry look good or swaying public opinion. Rather, he coached to build authentic Christ-followers, people who produced fruit. See Matthew 7:17.

• The Pharisees couldn't accurately assess themselves (Matthew 23:29-36).

The Pharisees didn't have accurate metrics to assess how well they were progressing in their "learning" organization. Their self-assessment indicated they were spiritually superior to the generations before them.

Jesus, however, knew that they were about to repeat the sins of their fathers.

Jesus' coaching involved honesty and a view with God's metrics. Humility was part of the package, as indicated in Matthew 5:3.

for discussion and reflection

1. Have you seen any modern day examples of the Pharisees' model of coaching and learning? What effect can it have on a ministry?

2. If you brought in Jesus as a consultant for your ministry, how do you think he'd coach you regarding your training model?

contemporary case study: karl "the kidologist" bastian

Karl Bastian is the children's pastor at the Village Church of Barrington, Illinois. Across North America, Karl is known as "The Kidologist" due to his extensive workshop speaking and kidology.org Web site.

Karl took the Dramatic Leadership Assessment Test and scored high in several styles, including Drama Coach. A veteran children's minister, Karl has learned to broaden the repertoire of his leadership style.

In fact, Karl attributes his effectiveness as a Drama Coach to his desire to be a lifelong learner. Surprisingly, Karl rarely schedules himself as a presenter at his own teacher training meetings.

"You know the verse about a prophet in his own country? Instead of presenting, I bring in outside experts to my teacher training meetings. Or I have one of my seasoned teachers present. They have so much wisdom."

Karl sits with his volunteers, takes notes, and asks questions. "My volunteers need to see me modeling being a learner. I can steer the conversation by asking questions, but it's important that they see me as a peer—learning."

Karl focuses the majority of his teaching ministry on his Leadership Team. The Leadership Team consists of the heads of each department in his children's ministry, and they meet each month. Karl opens each meeting with a question such as "If God gave you $1,000 to use in the children's ministry, what would you spend it on?"

Karl gives his team homework assignments, such as reading a leadership book together and discussing portions of it each month. He challenges his team to interact with the material and make personal applications.

According to Karl, creating a leadership team that values learning requires personal humility. "I need to convince my team that I'm a peer. That means that my ideas can die on the table, just like theirs can. I need to create an environment where people feel free to criticize me."

Once Karl showed his team a clip from the movie *First Knight,* where King Arthur established the Order of the Round Table. "Our meetings need to be just like that. There's no head of the table."

These meetings are valuable, but they are not Karl's preferred venue to exercise his teaching gift.

"My favorite way to teach is one-on-one. It took me awhile to learn that. It's easy to be happy in the spotlight. At my first ministry after Bible school, I launched the church's first kids' club and a children's church. Attendance tripled. However, I had to leave under difficult circumstances regarding the senior pastor.

"Our meetings need to be just like that. There's no head of the table."

"Ten years later, everything I put in place crumbled. Members look back at those days and refer to me as 'The Legend.' I look at all those years as a failure. All of the long hours and all-nighters that I spent to make that ministry sizzle—nothing remained.

"I ran the ministry instead of building it."

Today Karl sees one of his primary roles as being a coach for his leaders.

"I coach them how to solve their own problems. The answers to most problems are obvious to the paid professional. But I need to coach them through the 'big crisis,' then I need to let them do it. I'm not the paid fireman. I need to allow my leaders to lead."

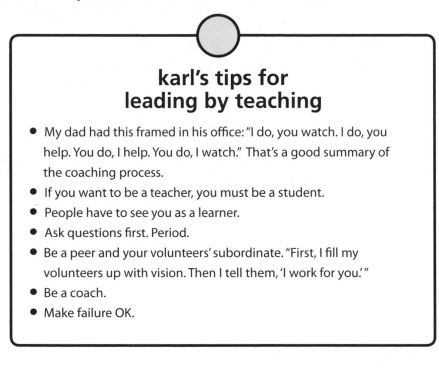

karl's tips for leading by teaching

- My dad had this framed in his office: "I do, you watch. I do, you help. You do, I help. You do, I watch." That's a good summary of the coaching process.
- If you want to be a teacher, you must be a student.
- People have to see you as a learner.
- Ask questions first. Period.
- Be a peer and your volunteers' subordinate. "First, I fill my volunteers up with vision. Then I tell them, 'I work for you.'"
- Be a coach.
- Make failure OK.

Karl uses his one-on-one coaching moments to give his leaders a vision that what they are doing is significant. "I want them to see a higher purpose for what they are doing."

Karl's method of leading through his leaders and building them up has paid off. Twice, when Karl moved on from a particular church, his teams were developed to the point where they were able to function without a paid children's minister. Both churches used that money to hire a staff person in a different department.

Karl sees his kidology.org Web site as an extension of his Drama Coach style. "It's a place where children's workers can swap ideas with each other and network. What breaks my heart is that there are *great* teachers out there that no one knows about. They teach a great object lesson once in front of 50 people and then it's lost.

"I want to create a place where we can learn from each other and recycle our best ideas."

The desire to be a lifelong learner drives Karl. "When I observe children's ministry professionals who are attached to outdated methods, I wonder if people will look at me someday and view me as dated. I need to constantly invent and reinvent myself so I'm always fresh."

how to be an effective drama coach— whether you are one or not

Whether you are a *natural* Drama Coach looking to sharpen your skills, or someone who just needs to *behave* like a Drama Coach, here's your step-by-step guide to success.

If leading by teaching doesn't come naturally to you, have no fear! One of the premises of this book is that you can *learn* any leadership skill and make it yours—if you are willing to pay the price.

Drama Coach, are you? Read this next section to sharpen your effectiveness as a teacher of teachers.

lessons from an ancient learning organization

I've mentioned that martial arts training is one of my hobbies. Originally, I got into the sport to get away from children's ministry. However, after a few years of training, I realized that tae kwon do is a metaphor for several leadership and discipleship principles.

In the past couple of decades, the concept of "learning cultures" has fascinated the business world. Books like *The Fifth Discipline* (by Peter M. Senge) fly off the shelves. However, tae kwon do is a learning culture that is older than Christianity.

Here's what I've learned about learning and teaching from tae kwon do.

• No matter how long you train, you're still a learner.

No one arrives. You begin as a white belt and progress through several levels until you become a black belt. However, becoming a black belt isn't the end of the road. There are *nine levels* of black belts that would take a lifetime to achieve.

I've taken a break from training because of a new baby and book writing. However, when I return to training, I know exactly where I'll be returning to in my learning—testing for my second-degree black belt. After that, I'll have just seven more degrees and…oh…50+ years ahead of me.

I'm convinced that we need to create a lifelong curriculum for our volunteers so they don't become bored or stagnant. Yes, there's turnover in every volunteer base, and the basics need to be covered regularly. But what about your longterm staff? Your long-timers need advanced training to keep children's ministry from becoming ho-hum.

Drama Coaches: It's up to *you* to create a culture in which everyone values learning.

Here are some tips that will keep you and your volunteers constantly learning...

* Get Children's Ministry Magazine into the hands of your key volunteers.

* Encourage your gifted volunteers to try their hand at writing curriculum. I have a seasoned teacher who now stays fresh in her teaching by writing for Group Publishing, Inc. Jan gets ongoing training from her editor in a way that I can't match.

* Read. I aim for this reading rotation each year: I read a business/management book, then a theology book, then something philosophical, then a good piece of fiction. Then I start back through the cycle.

It's important to stretch your mind by drinking from several streams of thought. My cycle might not work for you, and that's OK. The important thing is to make sure that you're being constantly challenged.

* Give blank VHS cassettes to 10 kids. Have them tape their favorite TV shows for you. Watch the shows and ask yourself, "Why does this show appeal to children?"

* Take up a new sport or hobby. The discipline of having to learn something new will pay dividends in your ministry.

* Invite parents and children to evaluate your ministry. Host a luncheon after church and invite parents to give input. Throw a pizza party on a kids' club night, and have children complete an evaluation of your ministry.

Drama Coaches: It's up to *you* to create a culture in which everyone values learning. As we learned in Karl Bastian's case study, *you* are the key player to make that happen.

• Progress is measured by your ability to teach.

The second "tae kwon do lesson" about learning organizations: Your personal progress is measured by your ability to teach.

My tae kwon do training began as an exercise in coercing my stiff body into unnatural positions and movements. Getting my body's cooperation felt like steering a car with elbows.

However, after several months, a strange thing happened. I realized I knew a few things. New people were joining the class, and they felt as lost as I had when I started. I reassured them that someday stretching would stop feeling like being dropped in a giant taffy machine.

I was able to help the new folks with the mechanics of basic kicks. I improved my own body mechanics through the discipline of being able to communicate them to others.

Mentoring is part of the fabric of tae kwon do. It's the responsibility of *every* higher belt to teach the lower belts, whether the task is memorizing new forms or sparring.

A black belt does not fight a colored belt to win. A black belt is a bear teaching a cub. The point is to cuff, not cudgel. A black belt's responsibility is to provide enough challenge so the lower belt struggles and grows in his or her ability to spar.

There's a time and place for all-out aggressive fighting. However, it's among your equals, and it never interferes with the learning environment.

Large group instruction is necessary. It's a major part of every class. However, the majority of the learning taking place in class is through the one-on-one training. During the second half of each class, you'll see green belts mentoring the yellow belts and brown belts bringing along the red belts. It's a chain of learning where everyone is assisting one another through the developmental stages of tae kwon do. It's this informal mentoring that creates black belts.

> **It's this informal mentoring that creates black belts.**

The higher your belt, the greater your responsibility is to be a teacher.

The more advanced you become as a leader, the greater your responsibility to mentor your team.

Here are some pointers to get you started…

• Lead a small group consisting primarily of your volunteers. Don't talk about children's ministry. Rather, focus on your team's spiritual formation.

• Develop a teacher-training program. Check out *Awesome Volunteers* by Christine Yount for a look at different models that thriving churches use.

• Imagine that you quit your role in children's ministry tomorrow. Which programs would still thrive and which would free-fall? Determine to mentor people to carry the programs you think would fall.

• Challenge your seasoned teachers to mentor new teachers. Consider placing new volunteers in with "master" teachers for the first three months of their volunteer placement.

• Create a buddy system during your teacher orientation. Pair off new teachers with experienced teachers. Encourage them to swap telephone numbers and e-mail addresses.

Remember the sign in Karl Bastian's father's office? Why not place it in yours?

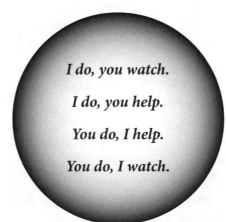

I do, you watch.

I do, you help.

You do, I help.

You do, I watch.

Mentoring isn't lecturing or classroom instruction. Mentoring is the life-to-life transference of experience, wisdom, and knowledge.

five-star teaching

Drama Coaches lead by teaching. But, what exactly are you supposed to *be* teaching to your volunteers and teams? Being really good at communicating the wrong stuff isn't going to help anyone.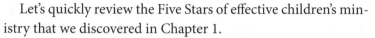

Let's quickly review the Five Stars of effective children's ministry that we discovered in Chapter 1.

• Star One: A Promised Land

Everyone needs to have a firm grasp on the Opening Night vision. If you have a Director on your team, work with that individual to come up with a strategy to keep the vision in front of your team.

Check out "How to be an effective director—whether you are one or not" on page 45 for ideas on how to embed the Opening Night vision in the minds of your church. It's wise to partner with your director to launch the vision.

After a new vision has been adopted, it needs to be constantly renewed and stirred. I have a church consultant friend, Steve Norris, who says that a vision will be forgotten in 28 days if it's not constantly renewed.

• Star Two: A Map

In Chapter 1 we discovered there are two kinds of maps—strategic plans and core values.

Is your team in the middle of a major transition? Then find out what parts of the plan are appropriate to share with the whole team. You can serve your Production Assistant by keeping "the map" in front of the team. You'll also give your team members a sense of security by keeping them in the loop.

The second kind of map is your ministry's core values. There's a fine line between these core values becoming your team's onboard navigation system and not just words.

Drama Coach, you're standing on that line. One of your roles as a Drama Coach is to create experiences that help your team understand how to make decisions based on these values.

• Star Three: A Well-Stocked Toolbox

Here's where a Drama Coach can shine! Remember that your children's ministry Toolbox is filled with the skills and competencies that volunteers need to possess in order to execute their roles effectively.

For example, Sunday school teachers need to know how to manage a classroom, use their curriculum, ask good debriefing questions, take attendance, follow up with new visitors, write accident reports, pray with children, lead a child to Christ… this list could go on all day.

Every team in your children's ministry has its own particular Toolbox needs. Your challenge is to be aware of what tools are needed by each team and to get the right tools in the right hands.

• Star Four: A Heart

The heart of your children's ministry is its set of collective emotions—the personality of your ministry. A healthy children's ministry heart is optimistic and joyful. Any conflict that bubbles up is dealt with in a Christlike manner.

That won't just happen. Drama Coaches need to teach their teams *how* to stay positive in the face of challenges. Drama Coaches can show teams how to be friendly to new visitors. Biblical models of conflict management need to be kept in front of the team.

As a Drama Coach, you can present the expectations for a heart-healthy children's ministry.

• Star Five: Muscle

Muscle, we've learned, is the get-it-done, sweaty work ethic of your ministry. As Drama Coach, lay out the expectation that team members will do what they say they will do. Influence others by being an example of servanthood. During training sessions, teach the benefits of getting it done. Inspire your teams to put themselves on the line.

create a training agenda

Wow. That's a lot of stuff to cover. Teaching toward a Five-Star ministry sets an impressive training agenda.

How do you know where to start? What topics should you lay out first? What can wait until later?

Here's my list of training issues, ranked in order of importance…

• Safety First

Any policy related to safe classrooms comes first. Teachers need to be schooled in the two-adult rule, evacuation procedures, accident reports, and universal precautions.

It doesn't matter how creative your classrooms are if a child gets hurt because of neglect on the part of one of your volunteers. Creativity won't count; it's lawsuit city. Train for safety during your initial teacher orientation.

• Vision

We've covered this in other places, so I'll simply mention that nothing keeps your volunteers in the game like a God-honoring vision. Constantly remind volunteers why they're doing what they're doing.

• The Felt Needs of the Volunteers

It makes sense to next train your teams in areas where they're ready to learn. Survey your teams and let them rank proposed training topics. If your volunteers are screaming for help in establishing discipline in their classrooms, teach on classroom management.

> **Nothing keeps your volunteers in the game like a God-honoring vision.**

• Strategic Agenda

Once you've ministered to your volunteers' felt needs, equip them to move forward. Train your volunteers to get to the Opening Night vision.

For example, when I first came to Grace, many of the teachers didn't value active learning. These teachers taught through rote memorization and teacher-focused lectures.

For the first four years of my ministry, I trained my teachers in active learning principles, along with safety issues, vision, and their

Five-Star Training Planner				
Choose One:				
Star 1: Promised Land	**Star 2: A Map**	**Star 3: A Well-Stocked Tool Box**	**Star 4: A Heart**	**Star 5: Muscle**
List the needed teaching objectives that will allow your team to reach the star.			**Curriculum Agenda**	**Coaching Agenda**
1)			What: When:	Who: When:
2)			What: When:	Who: When:
3)			What: When:	Who: When:
4)			What: When:	Who: When:

felt needs. I waited to get the signal that my team "got it" so we could move on.

Then, during a teacher training session, the vast majority of teachers took over and shared how they do active learning in their classrooms.

So I selected a *new* strategic training agenda. And I imagine it's going to take another three to four years before my ministry is known for its friendliness and ability to assimilate new visitors.

curriculum or coaching

You know *what* you want to teach and *when* you want to teach it. Now you need to decide *where* you want to teach it.

You need to determine whether a topic is best addressed in a classroom setting or in a one-on-one coaching situation. Or more likely, first in the classroom and then in a coaching situation.

Use the worksheet on the previous page to help map out your training agenda.

nontraditional teaching methods

A common frustration of Drama Coaches is getting your teams to show up for training opportunities. In fact, Keith Johnson, author of *Teacher Training on the Go,* says that the national average for attendance at children's ministry training events in the local church is 30 percent.

Ouch. That means seven out of 10 volunteers will probably never adequately get their Toolboxes filled. How can we fix that and equip more volunteers?

First, double-check to make sure you've removed the usual barriers to attendance by providing child care, convenient training times, delicious food, highly visible promotions, and high-quality training.

Then, after you've made sure to do everything in your power to build a crowd at your training sessions, it's time to go after the people who just can't or won't attend them.

Here are some ideas to get you started…

• E-mail

Send *brief* e-mails to your volunteers to cover a particular topic. Keep the content practical, simple, and did I mention brief? Consider using a simple Q and A format:

Q: I'm having a problem with parents dropping off their children late. It disrupts my preschool classroom when a child joins us 20 minutes after the service starts and then the child cries when his or her parents leave. What should I do?

A: *Dear Reader (Add your wise, practical, and brief answer here.) Include a brief affirmation to encourage your busy volunteers.*

• CD and Audiotape Trainings

This is an increasingly popular training format. Some children's pastors of larger churches' ministries are expanding their teaching ministry through tape or CD clubs. Some presenters allow you to make copies of their materials to distribute to your volunteers.[2]

• Internet

Enter "Children's Ministry" in your Internet Web browser, and you're off to the races! Several fantastic Web sites offer practical advice for children's ministry volunteers. Surf, find an article you enjoy, and e-mail the link to your volunteers.[3]

• Books and Magazines

Create a lending library of your favorite children's ministry books. If your budget allows, buy your key volunteers copies of Children's Ministry Magazine.

There you have it: How to be an effective Drama Coach—Whether You Are One or Not. Whether you're a natural Drama Coach or you're trying to play one through method acting, this leadership voice contains a powerful lesson for every leader.

Every effective leader must first be a learner. Without adopting the learning spirit of a Drama Coach, you quickly discover the ceiling of your leadership potential. As leaders, we will quickly reach the zenith of our potential unless we commit ourselves to continual discovery.

May God grant us all a double measure of childlike wonder.

the drama coach's prayer

Dear God,

Thank you for my leadership style. You have made my role one of passing wisdom, experience, and know-how from one generation of volunteers to the next. Give me the creativity to pass on a red-hot passion for you.

Make me an effective coach. Help me to correctly see what each volunteer and team member needs. Help me build winsome relationships with each person. Let joy be the carrier that transfers wisdom from me to the listener.

In Jesus' name, amen.

questions for reflection and discussion

1. How has your ministry benefited from the leadership of a Drama Coach?

2. Examine your children's ministry training regimen against the Five Stars. Which stars are being effectively addressed through training? Which stars need more of your attention?

3. What's the difference between classroom teaching and coaching? Does your children's ministry use a balance of both methods? How you can find balance?

Endnotes

1. Thom and Joani Schultz, *The 1 Thing™: What Everyone Craves—That Your Church Can Deliver* (Loveland, CO: Group Publishing, 2004).

2. Check out *Teacher Training on the Go* (Group Publishing). The discs included in the book are fantastic resources. I've used both the audio tracks and the e-mail blasts with my own teams. Good stuff!

3. Some of my favorite children's ministry Web sites are www.childrensministry.com, www.childrensministry.net, www.kidology.org, www.churchvolunteercentral.com, www.empoweringkids.net, and www.jimwideman.com. I'm not endorsing or agreeing with all of the content of any of these sites. However, I've found a ton of value by making regular stops to these sites.

CHAPTER (7)

the **theater manager**

"The Jones Family Versus Everyone Else: *A Melodrama by First Church."*

Debbie cringed at the thought, but if she'd been titling the musical accurately, that's the title she'd pick.

How could one family cause so much tension?

The Joneses were the all-American family. Both parents were successful professionals. The Mr. and Mrs. met and married while acting at the community theater, and Emily—their only child—was raised in the spotlights.

Emily was dragged to the theater to watch her parents rehearse until she was old enough to audition for the youth theater herself… and she'd landed her first part before she was in kindergarten.

The Joneses had just begun attending First Church after a neighbor invited them. Debbie wasn't quite sure where they were on their spiritual journey, but she had no question what journey they'd launched her on as a director.

The Joneses were taking her for a ride—her and everyone else attached to the musical.

Emily was an amazing actress. Debbie knew it. The children knew it. Emily knew it. And the Joneses knew it. Emily was head-and-shoulders above the other children when it came to stage presence.

However, Emily brought a lot of strain with her. It began with other children's parents resenting Mrs. Jones' expectation that Emily should just be handed the lead role. Emily earned the lead on merit, but some of the parents began to whisper.

Emily wasn't endearing herself to her peers either. She had a sharp tongue and was quick to point out the shortcomings of her novice counterparts. One of Debbie's weekly chores was to break up arguments among the children—arguments in which Emily was always involved.

Debbie's first instinct in dealing with the conflict was to focus on Opening Night.

"In three weeks it will all be over," she told herself with a sigh.

Tom wasn't so passive. Up until now, his only contribution to the team had been to buy snacks for the children.

However, Tom surprised Debbie and himself by taking over the rehearsal after the children started bickering again.

"Enough!" he said firmly.

The children stopped fighting. Without direction, Emily moved stage right while the rest of the cast moved stage left. Tom instructed the children to get into a circle, and they reluctantly shuffled together.

Tom told the children to talk about what was bothering them. He prodded Emily to express her frustrations with the cast without being mean. Debbie watched as Tom managed the communication, giving the children a chance to communicate better.

After 10 minutes, Tom concluded by saying, "Kids, we're doing this musical for God. We're doing it together. We're a team, and we are going to start acting like it.

"Emily, you know the most about acting. I want you to come to every rehearsal with one acting tip that you can share with your team. This is how you are going to serve others.

"Everyone, part of being a team is seeing the strengths in others. At the next rehearsal, we're going to spend 10 minutes talking about others' strengths. Come with something nice to say about everyone."

Tom turned the rehearsal back over to Dan and then sat next to Debbie.

"Sorry, if I was out of line by taking over, but I can't just watch these bad relationships without stepping in. The kids and their parents can't produce a musical for God while acting like the devil."

Debbie nodded in agreement. Was this the same guy who'd been bringing doughnuts?

"Debbie, we need to create a healthy and godly environment for the kids to work in if we're going to see the best results. We'd never have them rehearse in a room without heat or a room that was an absolute mess. But their spiritual and relational work space is a wreck."

Debbie took it all in before she spoke.

"You're our spiritual Theater Manager, Tom. It's now your job to keep bringing the snacks so kids can have time to build healthy relationships. But I also want you to bring a brief team-building exercise each week so the kids can develop Christian friendships.

"And I'll give you extra credit if you can work some of your magic with the parents!"

profile of a theater manager

In the world of drama, the Theater Manager provides a healthy environment in which everyone can work. Theater Managers pay the heating bills and make sure that the rehearsal rooms and stage are clean.

People work better in healthy working environments. By managing "the house," a Theater Manager leads by molding the attitudes of all the actors.

learning the parts If you think you might be a Theater Manager, reread the "Profile of a Theater Manager" again, this time with a highlighter pen in hand. The profile is a composite description of Theater Managers in general, but you know yourself best.

Customize the profile to fit yourself. Highlight sentences that your spouse or friends would point to and say, "No question about it—that fits you *perfectly!*" Place a star next to sentences that don't describe you at all.

If you know you *aren't* a Theater Manager, decide if you have a Theater Manager in your life. Does this description remind you of anyone in your church or children's ministry? Jot down the names of those people below.

_____

_____

_____

_____

In a ministry environment, the Theater Manager manages "the house" in which the rest of the team works. This house isn't built of brick and mortar. It's a house of emotions, attitudes, and relationships—each of which has a powerful influence on the health of the children's ministry.

That's because living in an environment of positive relationships gives you energy, while wading through a bog of negativity slows you down. It's the Theater Manager's job to lead by attending to your children's ministry's collective emotions.

Theater Managers are primarily motivated by the belief that healthy ministries flow from healthy teams and individuals, so Theater Managers constantly gauge the emotional and attitudinal health of their teams.

Theater Managers feel most satisfied when there's a positive sense of well-being among their team members. They enjoy tending to the personalities of their teams and ministries.

Theater Managers lead by guiding their teams through powerful emotional experiences that shape their teams' attitudes and morale. Theater Managers have a knack for uniting a diverse group of people into a common culture using training, symbols, experiences, and music.

Warning: Never think a Theater Manager is soft just because he or she is concerned about emotions. That's not the case at all.

Theater Managers become frustrated when they see team members exhibiting attitudes that harm the team's well-being. Theater Managers will go to the wall to defend the emotional vital signs of their teams, and they bare their teeth when leaders act without considering how their behavior will affect the team's morale.

A God-submitted Theater Manager upholds all five stars of children's ministry. By generating optimism, the Theater Manager gives the team the ability to chase the Promised Land concept and trust the Road Maps. By installing attitudes of perseverance and servanthood, the team is able to build both a Toolbox and Muscle. The Theater Manager monitors the quality of the relationships in the ministry, helping the corporate "heart" shine.

I'm not saying that the Theater Manager is that perfect leader we debunked in Chapter 1. However, the Theater Manager approaches leadership with a global perspective. He or she is the jack-of-all-trades.

Theater Managers are, after all, minding the house in which everyone else works.

Bible case study: THE APOSTLE PAUL

In the past year, I've come to see Paul in a new light. I'd always appreciated him as the master missionary who populated the Mediterranean with churches. Through three missionary journeys, he literally put Christianity on the map.

However, I'm beginning to appreciate the fact that Paul was also the cultural architect of each of those churches. He didn't wind them up and take off. Paul did his best to tend to the culture of each of those churches.

Each of Paul's letters to churches was an attempt to be a long-distance Theater Manager. Paul was incredibly disadvantaged in trying to care for the "relational house" of each church when he had only letter-writing for communication. Yet because of Paul's handicap, we can discover the qualities that mattered to Paul as he attempted to manage church culture.

Here are the big cultural themes, or core values, that I see popping up all over Paul's letters...[1]

• A culture of radical servanthood

Throughout Paul's writings, he's constantly calling church members to spend their lives serving one another. Paul writes that lifestyle servanthood is the only reasonable way to approach God (Romans 12:1-2). Paul holds up Jesus as the example of the ultimate servant (Philippians 2). Paul blesses the Thessalonians with a prayer that their culture would be known for its self-sacrificing love (1 Thessalonians 3:11-12).

Paul constantly worked to infuse the culture with a sense of optimism.

That's just a taste of Paul's teaching on servanthood. Paul was attempting to create a relational environment that would encourage God's people to live out their redemptive potential. What better way to live than in relationships where people were trying to draw that godly potential out of each other?

• A culture of indomitable hope

Several of the original churches suffered persecution from both Jewish missionaries and pagans who felt threatened by this "new religion." Paul constantly worked to infuse the culture with a sense of optimism. Paul evokes imagery of the church being a constantly conquering army (2 Corinthians 2:14). He calls his readers "more than conquerors" (Romans 8:37).

In Philippians, Paul reminds the flock that God finishes what he starts (Philippians 1:6). Paul taught a deterministic, unstoppable victory in God that nothing could derail (Romans 8:38-39).

Paul built a culture of optimism. No matter what a church saw swirling around it, the church was to be confident in God's abilities.

• A culture of unflagging perseverance

Building on optimism, Paul added a new core value: perseverance.

Perseverance is the ability to be productive no matter what difficulties are thrown at you. Throughout his writing Paul creates an expectation that struggle is a normal state for the church.

Paul praises the churches of Thessalonia for their ability to be birthed in the middle of the violent persecution that resulted in Paul being driven out of the city (2 Thessalonians 1:4).

Paul told a pastor-in-training to expect suffering (2 Timothy 3).

Paul built a practical theology of struggle to help the Corinthians understand how to use hard times as a way to strengthen their connection to Jesus (2 Corinthians 1:1-7).

Again, that's just a pinch of the verses about suffering with which Paul salts his letters. Paul was convinced that in order for Jesus' followers to "bear much fruit," Christ-followers needed to be able to thrive under pressure.

• A culture of inseparable interdependence

Paul wanted to create a church culture in which people couldn't live without each other. Paul laid out a doctrine of individual gifts being used to strengthen the whole body (1 Corinthians 12; Ephesians 4:14-16). He created metaphors from the worlds of agriculture and industry to help readers comprehend their interconnectedness (1 Corinthians 3:5-9).

Paul's motive was to create a church culture in which there were no Lone Rangers. Each person was given spiritual assets that everyone else needed. Paul wanted to see a connected community.

• A culture of collective righteousness

Part of the interconnectedness Paul envisioned was a sense of "corporate righteousness."

In mathematics, there's something called the "butterfly effect."

According to the theory, when a butterfly flaps its wings in South America, it can have an effect on the weather in New York City. Everything is interconnected, more powerfully than is usually recognized.

Paul knew this to be true in the spiritual word. "Private" behaviors of church members have an impact on the whole body. That's one reason Paul was so adamant about so-called private righteousness (Ephesians 5:1-5).

Paul taught that the fruit of the Spirit produced a yield that strengthened healthy relationships, while the fruit of the flesh yielded seeds of discord (Galatians 5:16-26).

Paul knew that the relational health of the whole body could be negatively impacted by the attitudes of a few (1 Corinthians 5:6-8). That's why Paul was so hawkish about *everyone* diligently protecting his or her own spiritual health and connection to God.

This is just a quick overview of the kind of culture Paul wanted to build into the church. Later in this chapter we'll catch glimpses of how Paul actually went about "theater managing" to build God's house.

for discussion and reflection

1. About which of Paul's core values do you feel most passionate? Why?

2. Why do you think Paul was so invested in the relationships and the emotional state of the churches he planted?

contemporary case study: craig jutila on golf, bowling, and culture

Craig Jutila is the Children's Pastor at Saddleback Church in California, one of the largest churches in America. Saddleback is also the epicenter of the Purpose Driven Model for church growth—one of the most widely used paradigms for church development. Listen in as I interviewed Craig…

LARRY: *What is culture?*

CRAIG: Culture is the way things are done. It's the vision, values, and behaviors of a group. Look, there are no written rules here in California that you can't paint your house pink if you want to. But no one does it. Why? It's not part of the culture.

Nowhere at Saddleback is it written, "You've got to be flexible," but it's part of our culture. I tell prospective staff, "You won't last six months if you aren't flexible." Even though it's not written down, it's how things are done.

This year during the Easter season we had to add another weekend service. This decision was made *the Wednesday before the service.* You've *got* to be flexible to make it in this culture.

LARRY: *Craig, rebut this objection: "I have many pressing things to do to get ready for Sunday. I don't have time to worry about our culture."*

CRAIG: People who think this way probably have an issue getting people to serve out of a sense of vision and not merely out of need. Scripture says, "Where there is no vision, the people perish" (Proverbs 29:18, King James Version).

Truth is, you're building a culture whether you know it or not. The issue is whether you are building a good culture or a poor culture.

LARRY: *What are some of the biggest threats to a healthy culture?*

CRAIG: Turnover. If you don't keep staff long-term, you can't build a culture well.

People need to be part of your team for about six years before they start to fully experience your culture. If someone stays on your staff six months or three years and then leaves, they never experience the benefit of being a part of the culture. If they could have just stuck it out a little bit longer, they would have experienced the payoff.

That applies to the turnover of volunteers also. Say your volunteers rotate through your children's ministry once a month. That's twelve times a year. They have *no* chance of assimilating your culture.

LARRY: *What are the "push buttons" that you use to get at your culture and shape it?*

CRAIG: Storytelling. Every culture needs those tribal storytellers who preserve the important milestones. Every healthy organization needs a historian.

Around here, one of our most important culture-building phrases is "remember when?" It's important that we take time to remember our history. It might be a time when a staff member got stuck in the basket of a cherry-picker machine, and we all had a good laugh. Or perhaps it was a time when we overcame a massive challenge.

"Remember when's" are important culture builders because they capture culture-defining, empowering moments.

Right now, in my office, I have a bucket filled with what looks like junk. It's not junk; it's history. There's a piece of Sheetrock from our old modular (the old children's ministry building). There's also a piece of concrete core pulled from the new building. On the wall, I have a framed registration sheet with the names of the first 50 children checked into the children's ministry on the opening day of the new kids' building. You can also see framed pictures of the first seven annual themes that we used to train our children's ministry volunteers.

> **"In my office, I have a bucket filled with what looks like junk. It's not junk; it's history."**

You also need to guard the health of your ministry. If you see a bad attitude, you need to go right after it. Recently I had too many staff members who weren't getting along. They started out antagonizing each other and then went to not talking to each other. I had to get them in my office and facilitate reconciliation. You can't let this stuff go on unchecked.

LARRY: *How do you go about getting your staff and volunteers to take ownership of your culture?*

CRAIG: I'd change that word *ownership* to *empowerment*.

It's like bowling. You tell your volunteers that they will be bowling in Lane 9. You don't get to choose the values, mission, or curriculum of the children's ministry. Those decisions are what make up Lane 9—and they've already been determined. But you give your volunteers freedom to bowl *within* that lane. You give them the ability to decide how to knock the pins down. You need to give your volunteers freedom to execute within a defined set of values.

LARRY: *What percentage of your workweek is involved in cultural architecture?*

CRAIG: Not that much anymore. Now I have a team that propagates the culture. But during the first six years I was at Saddleback, I was obsessed with the culture.

The first three years were very hard. I changed the music, several leaders, the curriculum, and a lot of the "how" and "why" of children's ministry—you know, those iconic things that no one wants to see messed with.

I actually had one parent tell me that they prayed that I would come under attack from Satan—that I would be the demise of children's ministry at Saddleback.

To change a culture that is ingrained takes an awful lot of octane. The first year I was at Saddleback, I listened. The second year, I rolled out the plan. The third year, we began to execute that plan. It took an amazing amount of octane to change the culture of this ministry.

You have to be so careful with your culture. It's like golf. You can control your swing, but once the ball takes off—it's over. There's nothing more you can do but watch. It takes more octane to redo a culture than it does to build it right the first time.

how to be an effective theater manager—whether you are one or not

Maybe you're a natural Theater Manager. Perhaps you've been trained to be strong in this area. Either way, this section will help you achieve a personal Promised Land—you can increase your effectiveness as a Theater Manager.

If you're a natural Theater Manager, you'll know it in your gut by the end of this chapter.

If you aren't, you might leave this chapter feeling frustrated. That's OK. Hang in there, and you'll still glean some great leadership ideas.

The reason this style can be so nebulous is that the Theater Manager's job is to lead something you can't see, taste, or touch: culture.

Culture is invisible but real. And it's *really* powerful. It's too big to ignore. Leaders refer to culture different ways. I've heard culture described as "the vibe," "an atmosphere," or "an ethos."

When I worked in the children's mental health field, we defined a family culture as the values, traditions, beliefs, and attitudes that determine how family members behave and express themselves.

Let's use that definition to talk about our ministries, too. Our children's ministries have cultures made up of the values, traditions, beliefs, and attitudes that determine how team members behave and express themselves.

Not only does your children's ministry have a culture, but that culture *matters*...

• Children's ministries always underachieve if they believe they are understaffed due to senior leadership neglecting them.

• Children's ministries that exude relational warmth tend to keep visitors.

• Children's ministries that celebrate how God worked in the past tend to expect God sightings in the future.

• Children's ministries filled with whiny, complaining volunteers don't attract more volunteers.

You see, culture is a *powerful* thing. While it may be invisible, it's also inescapable. Someone needs to take responsibility to shape your children's ministry culture.

If you choose to accept this mission, that someone is you.

Here are some steps you can take toward being an artful Theater Manager...

determine what your children's ministry culture is today

Before you can get your relational house in order, you need to have a firm grasp on its condition. It's a subjective call, but you can zero in on some concrete findings. Here are some techniques that will be helpful:

• Use anonymous surveys to find out what your volunteers feel about the ministry. Poll those volunteers to find out what they love and hate about being a children's ministry volunteer.[2]

• Ask parents to tell you what they like about your children's ministry and what frustrates them. Ask them to choose a word or two that describe the children's ministry.

• Throw a pizza party for the children. Have kids write or draw pictures of what they love about coming to church. Allow the kids to tell you what they can live without.

• Pick three words or phrases that best describe how your volunteers relate to each other. What comes to mind? "Teamy" or "unconnected"? "Harmonious" or "conflicted"?

• Look at your ministry's written core values. Do they reflect your culture? If you had a strong emotional reaction to any of those values, ask yourself if that emotion points to a disconnect between "reality" and "what's only on paper."

determine your ideal culture

Once you know the reality of your culture, it's time to decide if you want it to change and, if so, what it will look like.

To what cultural ideals is your church aspiring? Excellence? Friendliness? Servanthood? Make those your own.

• First, look at your church's core values. To what cultural ideals is your church aspiring? Excellence? Friendliness? Servanthood? Make those your own. Revisit Chapter 3, and rethink whether your children's ministry aligns with your big church.

• Dust off your ministry-specific core values. Do they reflect what you *really* want to build?

• Host a brainstorming meeting with your key volunteers. Have them dream about what the ideal children's ministry culture would look like. Write their ideas down on a piece of newsprint. Have them rank the top five attributes that they think the children's ministry should embody.

• Study the Word. Look for clues as to the kind of culture that Jesus, Paul, and others attempted to build during their ministries. Write them down.

• Pray. Ask God to tell you where to start.

cultural acupuncture

You know your real culture, your ideal culture, and the gap between the two. It's time to be about the business of shaping your culture! But be aware: Designing a culture isn't a linear, step-by-step, enterprise.

It's more like acupuncture.

Have you ever seen an acupuncturist at work? The client lies on a table, his or her body sprouting long needles. Those who subscribe to acupuncture believe that by placing needles at the right pressure points, health can be restored to the body.

Like acupuncture, culture shaping requires that pressure be simultaneously applied at several strategic points of your children's ministry's culture. Here are some of the "needles" you'll need in your toolbox…

• Affirmation

You have the power to breathe energy and courage into a volunteer merely by thanking him or her for a job well done. Through a card, a telephone call, or a small gift, you can encourage positive behaviors that embody the highest hopes for the culture.

• Celebration

Celebrate milestones together! Each May, I throw a dinner for all the volunteers and cook a gourmet meal for them. At the end of the night, we swap stories about how God moved in our children's ministry. As the stories of life-change pile up, the volunteers leave with a renewed sense of purpose, vision, and determination. Their work matters! Who doesn't need to see that?

Celebrate successful events in the "big church." Take pictures of every event throughout the year. During the announcements, project the highlights from your event in front of the congregation and praise your volunteers. Talk about why this event had eternal significance in the lives of children.

Celebration breeds optimism. So party on!

• Narration

I've already mentioned the power of storytelling. A masterful Theater Manager always has a handful of stories to tell.

The first story you need to be able to tell is "The Story of How Your Children's Ministry Connects With God's Story." This story infuses culture with energy and purpose.

Here's an example of how I tell this story at Grace. I call it "A Brief History of the World in Three Acts."

ACT ONE

Sin enters the world. Three friendships are broken…
- Humanity's friendship with God.
- Humanity's friendship with each other.
- Humanity's friendship with the world.

ACT TWO

Jesus comes to earth and give two rules…
- Have a great friendship with God.
- Have a great friendship with each other.

Jesus then dies on the cross to give us the power to obey these rules.

ACT THREE

BridgeKids Ministry (our children's ministry) helps kids…
- Build a friendship bridge to God through worship.
- Build a friendship bridge to the church through service.
- Build a friendship bridge to the world through outreach.

THE END

That story pumps purpose into the veins of our culture by connecting the weekly grind of preparing a Sunday school lesson to our redemptive history.

Next, we tell stories of biblical kids who build these three bridges. Our culture needs to believe that God has worked and does work through children when he wants to get things done.

It's my job to place the stories of Samuel, David, Rhoda, Ishmael, Naaman's servant girl, and the "fish-and-bread boy" in front of every child and adult in the church. They need to be to reminded that throughout history, God uses kids to be bridge builders.

Finally, I need to have a fresh story or two in my pocket that tell how our children are building bridges. It might be Kara building a bridge to the world by taking a musical tape to her public school to share with her class, or Alex leading a child to Christ in the lunchroom.

It might be the story of delighted senior citizens enjoying a visit from the "Can Do Kids," our children's ministry outreach and service team.

Or it may be the story of how elementary kids served the preschoolers by making modeling dough.

What are the stories of your culture? You have them. Carefully select the stories that will give your culture energy, and intentionally start sharing those stories.

A Theater Manager needs to be willing to inspect, evaluate, and enforce the culture.

• Evaluation

Theater Managers can't get by just by partying and swapping stories. There's a harder side to their roles. Worthy Theater Managers inspect their ministries and then enforce their culture.

What good is having a core value of friendliness if your volunteers aren't getting there on time? What's the point of a core value of excellence when your teachers come to class unprepared to teach the lesson?

What's the point of valuing teams, only to have volunteers engage in gossip and backstabbing?

A Theater Manager needs to be willing to inspect, evaluate, and enforce the culture. That's true even if it means having a hard conversation with a teacher.

Your volunteers need to know that you care enough about your culture to protect it. Quite frankly, you can't expect them to care more about the culture than you do.

So let them know that you care by gently calling them to task when a reminder is merited.

• Quality Communication

Nothing chokes the health of a culture like ungodly communication. Paul spilled a lot of ink policing the communication habits of the early churches. Read Ephesians 4:25-32.

Unhealthy communication siphons energy away from the God-work and wastes it in conflict. A runaway conflict can take down a ministry or even a whole church.

It nearly happened to the church where I serve.

After moving through a significant change process that was making our 100-plus-year-old church young again, the staff, elders, and congregation found themselves hopelessly divided about nearly everything.

I can't begin to describe the stress our culture felt. Personally, I didn't sleep well for months, lost weight, and was perpetually sullen. I think that would be an apt description for our culture as well.

We hired a professional Christian conflict mediator to come in and lead us through a painful process of dialogue and repentance, and through that process we became healthy again. We lost one paid staff person through the process, but that individual remains at our church and serves as a volunteer.

The church where I serve—Grace—is a miracle. By all human standards, we should be a small, wounded church struggling to make ends meet. Instead, we're a growing testament to God's goodness. We're a living warning about the dangers of ungodly communication and a testament that God can redeem any situation.

There are few things more important than shepherding the quality of communication in your ministry. If you want to build culture-strengthening communication skills in your ministry, read Craig Jutila's *The Growing Leader*. It's an excellent tool you'll put to good use.

• Branding

The last "needle" you'll need for cultural acupuncture is "branding" your ministry in much the same way a sports equipment company creates an identity for products. Metaphors, images, and music are powerful tools to galvanize your culture and create a distinguishable brand.

I've come to believe that branding is a core leadership function that can't be ignored.

You draw your volunteers from diverse walks of life. Each of your volunteers has a plate already loaded with family, bills, hobbies, and careers. They lead separate lives that seldom if ever intersect.

How do you create a common culture when the people in your children's ministry see one another just hours every week?

You do this with...

• Metaphors

Give your people a common word picture to wrap their minds around. At Grace, we use the metaphor of a bridge. We make connections between the shores of who we are and who God is. We make friendship bridges with each other and our neighbors.

This bridge metaphor helps our people bias themselves toward being people who build connections. During the release of Mel Gibson's *The Passion of the Christ,* Pastor Mike booked five theaters for private viewings. We estimated that 500 of our people invited 800 of their co-workers and friends to the film.

> **Give your people a common word picture to wrap their minds around.**

However, when a local parachurch organization lobbies our people to go and boycott or picket something, only handfuls of our people go out and do it.

Why? Because that behavior isn't suggested in our metaphor. It's not a part of our culture. We're bridge builders, not bridge blockers.

What's your ministry's metaphor? If you don't have one, it's time to start kicking the idea around with your team. The Bible is full of word pictures that can energize and define your culture.

• Images

What do the Nike "Swish," a swastika, a hammer and sickle, and the cross have in common? They are powerful images that instantly evoke powerful emotions in the hearts of their viewers.

Your ministry needs a logo. Commission a local artist to create one for you, or ask a capable person in your church to help. And don't think money is an obstacle. There are plenty of free logo generators on the Internet that can get you in the game.

• Music

Music is powerful. A certain song playing in a passing car can pull you right back into vivid memories of your high school or college days.

Music can prompt emotions, evoke worship, and summon a people for action.

Music can define a movement.

You can't even *think* of Billy Graham Crusades without mouthing the words to "Just As I Am."

Hear "Eye of the Tiger" on an oldies station and the *Rocky* movies come to mind.

John Wimber built the Vineyard Movement as much with his guitar as with his preaching.

You can shape your culture by carefully selecting music that helps define who you are. If your group aspires to communicate the gospel to kids in a contemporary fashion, then by all means pipe the latest, greatest kids' worship music through your hallways.

I've been blessed to have a skilled kids' worship leader/songwriter on the team. Bill Mason is a former punk rocker from England who leads my elementary children's church team. A few years ago I challenged him to start recording a worship album.

The *Run to the Lord* album was the result of that challenge. Those songs capture our culture somehow—we're contemporary and quirky.

The kids and the church rallied around that music. It's been one of the greatest momentum builders we've ever experienced. We're currently in the studio working on the follow-up album.

Why?

Because we firmly believe that this next album will help further set our brand and help define our culture.

Maybe you aren't in a place where you can make your own CD. However, you can shop for music that champions core values such as servanthood and excellence. Build that music into your training events.

You *can* build a soundtrack for your movement.

So there are your "needles" for cultural acupuncture. You can improve your culture by using one or a handful of these needles. However, with practice, you'll get to the point where you simultaneously work multiple pressure points in your culture to promote maximum health.

And a healthy children's ministry is a productive children's ministry.

May God use you to help your ministry experience the abundant life!

a theater manager's prayer

Dear God,

You've given me a passion for the church—the body of Christ. You've given me a passion for the body to be healthy and robust. Help me promote healthy relationships, attitudes, and beliefs in the body.

Make our ministry harmonious, industrious, and optimistic. May we honor you by owning not only your goals but your personality as well.

In Jesus' name, amen.

for reflection and discussion

1. How would you describe the culture of your children's ministry?

2. What "needles" are you currently using to promote a healthy culture? What "needles" can you add to your quiver?

3. Who on your team can start championing the health of your children's ministry culture?

Endnotes

1. This section could be a book of its own. If you want to dig deeper in this area, e-mail me at leadthewayGodmadeyou@earthlink.net, and I'll e-mail you the file in which I recorded my Bible study on Paul.

2. www.churchvolunteercentral.com has some excellent sample surveys that will help you understand your team's attitudes and beliefs about volunteerism in your church.

CHAPTER (8)

the **stagehand**

'Twas the night before the dress rehearsal.
Bleary-eyed, Debbie headed off to the church. She'd just tucked her kids into bed and had a late night ahead of her.

The costumes needed to be hung in the changing room. Props needed to be laid out in the correct order…decorations hung in the hallways…programs folded…and the list went on.

Debbie was bone-aching tired. The past three months of this musical had been wonderful but exhausting. Debbie reflected on all of the leadership lessons she'd learned from her team.

Patricia taught her how to strategize.

Susie taught her how to organize.

Dan taught her how to equip her team.

Tom taught her how to unify her team.

Debbie pulled into the church parking lot and thought,

"Leadership lesson, number 52: Recruit some help before the big event."

She unlocked the church door and pushed back thoughts of resentment. "Why am I the only one here?"

To her surprise, she wasn't.

Someone had hung all of the costumes and labeled them with the children's names in large print.

The props were laid out neatly on a table, just offstage. They were arranged in order of when they'd be needed in the musical.

Debbie heard the copier and set off to see who the angel was.

Steve was at the copier, back turned to her, folding programs and placing them in a pile. He didn't hear Debbie approach because of the music blaring through his headphones.

Debbie watched while Steve cheerfully folded to the beat of the music.

"What a servant," she thought. "I'd have been here all night."

Steve sensed Debbie standing behind him. Startled, he spilled a handful of programs on the floor.

Debbie quickly bent to pick up the programs as Steve pulled off his headphones and knelt beside her.

"Wow, Steve. I thought I was going to be here all night. Hey, I thought you were going to be out of town tonight."

"I was," Steve shrugged. "Plans changed so I thought I'd come by and pitch in and take care of some of the chores. I'm almost done. What else do you need?"

"I think we're done for tonight. Thanks so much, Steve."

"No problem. You get some rest. I'll get here early to open the doors and make the coffee. Send me an e-mail if you think of anything else."

Steve paused, then put the folded programs on a countertop. He cleared his throat. "Look, I don't want you worrying about this stuff. I'm a behind-the-scenes kind of guy so I'll handle the busywork. You focus on directing tomorrow. It's going to be a great musical, you know. I'm happy to help in any way I can."

On her way out of the church, Debbie poured her coffee down the sink.

She smiled to herself. "I guess I won't be needing that."
Within 15 minutes, Debbie was back home, in her pajamas,
ready to get a full night's sleep before Opening Night.

profile of a stagehand

Steve is a Stagehand. In the theater, a Stagehand advances a team's
progress by meeting the physical needs of the team. Stagehands build
the sets and make sure the props are acquired and in working order.

In a ministry setting, Stagehands serve their teams through acts
of service. Stagehands are interested in meeting the physical needs of
their ministry teams. They're amazingly flexible and willing to plug
themselves into any hole that needs to be filled.

Stagehands are often able to anticipate what supplies and labor the
team needs to accomplish its goals and can take steps to solve problems before they are noticed by others.

Stagehands usually would rather be of assistance to the team members on the front line than to be in the spotlight themselves. They enjoy
working behind the scenes to support the more visible team members.

Stagehands take pride in their willingness to do whatever it takes to
get the job done.

Where can you spot a Stagehand? Stagehands tend to volunteer for
the set up and tear down phases of most events. You'll find them wherever there are jobs that are menial but which must be accomplished
with excellence. Stagehands lead by serving. They know that these jobs
could pile up and get in the way of the team accomplishing its goals.

You might find a Stagehand leading a Sunday school class, or helping in the nursery, even when they don't believe they are gifted teachers. To a Stagehand, need dictates their method of service.

The flexibility of a Stagehand can take a toll. Stagehands sometimes
find themselves feeling forgotten or taken advantage of by the rest of the
team. Stagehands can be judgmental of team members who overlook
the physical or less visible jobs that need to be done in the ministry.

At times, Stagehands can find themselves in a ministry position for
which they aren't naturally suited. Their drive to meet needs can lead

149

learning the parts If you think you might be a Stagehand, reread the "Profile of a Stagehand" again, this time with a highlighter pen in hand. The profile is a composite description of Stagehands in general, but you know yourself best.

Customize the profile to fit yourself. Highlight sentences that your spouse or friends would point to and say, "No question about it—that's you!" Place a star next to sentences that don't describe you at all.

If you know you *aren't* a Stagehand, decide if you have a Stagehand in your life. Does this description remind you of anyone in your church or children's ministry? Jot down the names of those people below.

_____

_____

_____

_____

them into potentially frustrating situations.

Yet in spite of those risks, the Stagehand is the prince of leadership voices. God-honoring Stagehands lead in the spirit of their savior, Jesus. They inspire every style of leader to deny their own interests and make the church beautiful.

Stagehands specifically uphold the Muscle ministry star. Stagehands lead by getting things done and removing obstacles. Typically, they lead by tackling the dirty work, allowing the more visible team leaders to shine.

Bible case study of a stagehand: PHOEBE THE MISSIONARY

At the end of his letter to the Romans, Paul instructs the church to welcome a missionary he is sending to them…

"I commend to you our sister Phoebe, a servant of the church in

Cenchrea. I ask you to receive her in the Lord in a way worthy of the saints and to give her any help she may need from you, for she has been a great help to many people, including me" (Romans 16:1-2).

We don't have much information about Phoebe. She shows up only in these two verses. But there are some key clues in these verses that tell us how she led with the Stagehand voice...

• Paul calls her a deacon.[1]

The noun Paul uses to describe Phoebe is Greek word *deaconia*. It's a form of the same noun that is used in Acts 6 to describe the seven men who are generally identified as the first deacons.

Hey, before you run that last sentence through your theological and denominational grids, remember this: Back then, there were no deacon *boards*. This isn't about who's governing the church. It's an account of who was actually leading the church...by serving.

Phoebe exercised her leadership prowess by, in Paul's words being "a great help to many people." Phoebe got things done. We don't know exactly what she did, but we can infer from the Romans 16 passage, that she took care of the practical needs so Paul could focus on his teaching ministry.

• Paul valued her leadership enough to send her as a missionary.

Paul viewed Phoebe as a strategic kingdom player. Apparently, he didn't identify anyone among the churches in Rome with the same availability and servanthood capacity as Phoebe. So he invited her to journey to Rome to lead in his absence.

• Paul expected the Roman churches to roll out the red carpet for Phoebe.

Paul told the Romans in plain language to give her a special welcome. Whenever Paul sent a strategic leader into one of his church plants, he expected that church to welcome that leader with honor.[2]

Paul told the Romans to help her in any way she asked of them. Paul was lending the church a tremendous servant leader, and they were to treat her as such. Phoebe was a get-it-done leader.

And Paul was confident that the Roman church would be stronger for his sending her to them.

---

for discussion and reflection

1. Why do you think Paul valued Phoebe's servant leadership so highly?

2. Who on your children's ministry team has Phoebe-like qualities? How have you honored that person?

---

contemporary case studies: two of my terrific teammates

In our modern world, churches hire professional children's ministers. And while I guess that makes sense, I'm thrilled that churches aren't in the habit of hiring "professional volunteers." That's because when I came to Grace I inherited two amazing Stagehands, Craig and Irene.

And quite frankly, I don't know what I'd do without either one of them.

Craig is pure Stagehand. He's never seen a need that he didn't seriously consider meeting himself.

Every year we update our children's church stage to get ready for our new adventure. We've had time machines, spaceships, jungle scenes, spy headquarters—you name it. Each time we've redone the set, Craig is there with his tool belt and circular saw, ready to pitch in.

Craig is also on the children's church team, but he doesn't like being the "top banana." He's more comfortable being part of the ensemble than being the main character who's leading the program.

Says Craig, "I'm content letting Captain Bill have the limelight. I'm just there to help Bill out. In fact, when Bill retires, I'm retiring too."

Craig has served "The Captain" for over 10 years. Quite frankly, I don't see either one of them retiring. They're having too much fun together. And during that whole decade they've been together, Craig has craved the role of Stagehand.

Craig has also been a pinch hitter over the years. Craig has happily filled in as a teacher in classes of all ages, whether the reason is a recruiting shortfall or a sick teacher. While Craig has become a skilled teacher from all his years as a children's ministry volunteer, that's not what motivates him.

Craig has the heart of a Stagehand. And whether he knows it or not, he's been a leader. He's been an example of a "whatever-it-takes" attitude.

Through Craig's modeling, the servanthood index has been raised all throughout the BridgeKids Ministry.

And then there's Irene. She's the perfect example of a leader who is completely submitted to God and who allows the Stagehand leadership style to transform her primary style—Stage Manager.

Irene is an organizer. When I had our team members fill out a personal profile page, she listed "making lists" among her hobbies. For roughly a decade, Irene has brought order to our nursery ministry. The schedules, the reminder cards—you name it, nothing escapes her eye for detail.

I love Irene's organizational ability. She approaches leadership from an absolutely different starting place than I do, but do you know what? It's not her organizational skills that make her an invaluable part of my team. It's her servanthood.

When I first came to Grace, she introduced herself as the nursery coordinator. What she failed to mention is that she has a Master of Divinity degree and a Ph.D. in psychology. Irene has more relevant education than almost every pastor on our staff! I think it took me over a year to figure that out.

Early on, Irene served me by having a hard conversation with me. She pointed out to me that my ministry was disorganized.

I have to admit that at first blush I didn't *feel* served, then I realized she was right. I was trying to build a playground of creativity in which the kids would fall in love with God.

Irene let me know that instead I was building a swamp. Until

I drained away all of the disorganization and built the systems that would create trust among the volunteers and parents, I had no chance of meeting my goals.

Next, Irene served me by helping me build these systems. She spent the next several months helping me create and review the policies that still serve us today.

Irene could have zapped me with a "hit-and-run" criticism. And you know what? I would have deserved it. My systems *did* stink at the time. However, through her Stagehand's heart, she led.

Our children's ministry is a much stronger, welcoming, and secure place due to Irene's leadership. And through Irene's servanthood, I've learned how to think like a Stagehand also. That's no small feat for me to have accomplished.

So Irene and Craig, let me thank you again right here. Without your servant leadership, BridgeKids wouldn't be as effective as it is today. And chances are this book would never have been written!

Craig, without you I'd be building sets instead of writing. And you know how unhandy I am!

And Irene, I'm convinced that you supplied me with the Children's Ministry 101 education I never had. I'm not sure I'd still be in the game without you being you.

Thank you both so much for leading by serving.

how to be a stagehand—whether you are one or not

Whether you're a *natural* Stagehand looking to sharpen your skills, or someone who just needs to *behave* like a Stagehand, here's your guide to success.

This guide is going to look radically different from any of the others you've read so far. The other five leadership styles can be mastered through practicing technique and method.

The Stagehand leadership voice requires a change of *heart*—an admission that the greatest thing that we can do with our lives is to lose ourselves in the pursuit of serving others.

Whatever it takes.

Whatever it forces you and me to do.

Fortunately, there's no seven-step outline to accomplish that.

Yes, I said *fortunately*. God did endow some of us with a supernatural capacity to serve (Romans 12:7). However, for the rest of us, achieving the lifestyle of a Stagehand is a lifelong battle that forces us to confront our self-centeredness.

If you are a natural Stagehand, may this section affirm you and inspire you to continue leading your children's ministry through servanthood.

For the rest of us, I suggest that we look at the following pages devotionally and ask God to transform our leadership styles.

the stagehand style transforms every other leadership voice

The Stagehand style is a leadership voice in its own right. However, combined with any of the other five styles, it transforms those styles.

Any of these leadership voices that we studied can be bent and deformed so that *our* goals are met instead of God's. The Stagehand voice anchors these styles in the nature of God. Good leaders become *great* leaders in God's eyes.

• Nehemiah: A Transformed Director/Production Assistant

Take a quick look at Nehemiah's career, and you can see strong Director and Production Assistant tendencies. Nehemiah had a vision for a rebuilt Jerusalem and knew how to build a strategy to get the job done.

However, Nehemiah was also a humble servant. He became credible to the people he was trying to lead by serving them. During the construction of the city walls, Nehemiah not only built the watch-guard schedule, he also took his turn watching the walls during the night shift (Nehemiah 4:22-23).

When Nehemiah was elevated to the office of Governor, he refused to take the governor's allowance of food or money. These were hard times, and Nehemiah refused to assert his rights at the expense of his people (Nehemiah 5:14-16).

Through his servanthood, Nehemiah won the hearts of the people, rebuilt Jerusalem, and supervised the repatriation of the nation.

Not too shabby.

• Ezra: A Transformed Drama Coach

Nehemiah's counterpart, Ezra, was a die-hard Drama Coach…

"…because the good hand of his God was upon him. For Ezra had set his heart to study the law of the Lord and to practice it, and to teach his statutes and ordinances in Israel" (Ezra 7:9b-10, NASB).

Ezra wasn't content with merely sharing his wealth of information with Israel.

Ezra was also a Stagehand. His teaching was an act of service, and his passion was that his people would experience life transformation. Ezra knew his people were at odds with God and wanted his teaching to serve his people so they could live as the people of God.

Through his servanthood, Nehemiah won the hearts of the people.

In Chapter 9, we hear Ezra's Stagehand voice clearly. He's just led a large caravan of his people out of Babylon back to Israel. Ezra learns that his people have fallen back into some of the sinful patterns that led to their predicament.

Ezra could have relied on his teaching skills and browbeat Israel. It was within his rights. However, Ezra goes to the temple and *weeps* for his people (Ezra 9:5-15). He serves his people through an impassioned intercessory prayer to God.

The nation is moved by Ezra's servanthood. In Chapter 10:1, we see revival spontaneously taking place. A large crowd wells up around the temple and joins Ezra in his prayer for the nation.

What was at stake here? God judging the nation a second time for their unfaithfulness, even before they can get their bags unpacked from the first exile. Ezra's humble Stagehand behavior saved the nation.

• Joseph: The Transformed and Forgiving Stage Manager

We took an in-depth look at Joseph the Stage Manager in Chapter

5. However, we'd be remiss not to take a second glance to see how a Stagehand voice guided his behavior.

When Joseph was in prison, he served two imprisoned officials of Pharaoh by interpreting their dreams.

Why?

These weren't *his* people. They were his captors. Why would he help them?

When Joseph was brought before Pharaoh, he served Pharaoh by interpreting his dream.

Why? Joseph was most *definitely* the Pharaoh's captive.

When desperation drove his brothers into his reach, Joseph rejected any impulse to extract revenge. Instead, Joseph made sure that his family was cared for.

Why? His brothers had betrayed him.

Joseph had the heart of a Stagehand. He knew that his life was not about himself. Rather, Joseph lived a life of service to fulfill God's purposes.

• Paul: The Transformed Theater Manager/Slave

Paul, the master church planter and Theater Manager, had a heavy measure of Stagehand in him, too. Instead of always asserting his authority as an apostle, Paul's business card read: "Paul, a bond slave of Jesus Christ."

That's how he saw himself—owned by Jesus and at Jesus' service.

In fact it was Paul's willingness to serve at Jesus' disposal that laid some significant foundation blocks of the church.

Occasionally Paul had to trot out his credentials for the churches. False teachers often attempted to make themselves seem credible by presenting an impressive theological pedigree.

Here are the credentials that Paul flashed to the Corinthian churches when they questioned his apostleship…

"Rather, as servants of God we commend ourselves in every way: in great endurance; in troubles, hardships and distresses; in beatings, imprisonments and riots; in hard work, sleepless nights and hunger" (2 Corinthians 6:4-5).

Paul believed that no amount of hardship was beneath him in order to build the church. Without his servanthood, all of Paul's "cultural ar-architecture" would largely have been theoretical, and there would have been far fewer congregations waiting to hear from him.

Why is it so important that you make the Stagehand style your own?

This style causes self-forgetfulness. It's so easy to get enamored with our gifts and our leadership. But that's a dangerous place to be.

It's been said, "When all you have is a hammer, everything looks like a nail."

Let me tweak that a bit: "When we become infatuated with our own gifts and leadership voices, we tend to distort every situation into a chance to showcase our own assets."

We forget that God gave us our gifts for the good of *others*.

Directors: *God gave you your gift so your team can find direction.*

Production Assistants: *God gave you your style so your team can find strategy.*

Stage Managers: *God gave you your style so your team can be efficient.*

Drama Coaches: *God gave you your style so your team can be effective.*

Theater Managers: *God gave you your style so your team can be healthy.*

Stagehands: *God gave you your style to remove obstacles so other leaders can do their thing.*

Leadership is about *others*. Not you. Not me.

> It's been said, "When all you have is a hammer, everything looks like a nail."

Friend, determine to desire the Stagehand style at all costs. At some point in your development as a godly leader, you will get to a point of decision: Are you doing this for yourself or for Jesus?

There *will* come a point where submitting your leadership gift to God is going to cost you more than you ever bargained for. I guarantee it.

Building the Stagehand style into the fabric of your leadership now won't make the crossroads any less painful later. However, you will choose the correct path—the one that drives you to servanthood…and your team to growth.

servanthood mirrors Jesus' ministry

The Stagehand leadership voice is central because it transforms the other leadership styles. No other leadership style captures the heart of Jesus' ministry like this one.

"The Son of Man did not come to be served, but to serve, and to give his life as a ransom for many" (Matthew 20:28).

Stagehands lead like Jesus did: Their priority is to meet the needs of others.

• Bottom of the Pile

I think I discover the truths of Scripture best when I'm trying to teach them to children. The process of presenting a Scripture at a child's level forces me to really think about what a verse means.

This recently happened to me with 1 Peter 2:4-6...

"As you come to him, the living Stone—rejected by men but chosen by God and precious to him—you also, like living stones, are being built into a spiritual house to be a holy priesthood, offering spiritual sacrifices acceptable to God through Jesus Christ. For in Scripture it says: 'See, I lay a stone in Zion, a chosen and precious cornerstone, and the one who trusts in him will never be put to shame.' "

What's going on in these verses?

We, the church, get to be "living stones." We're given the privilege of joining together to make up a "living temple." The gifts we offer to God are acceptable because of Jesus.

This, my friend, is a pretty good deal. Especially when you consider where Jesus is standing in this picture.

Jesus is standing at the bottom of the pile. He's the rock holding everyone up.

Jesus is called the "rejected" stone, *rejected* being a one-word reference to the passion and crucifixion of Christ.

Jesus served us in his suffering and by being our perfect sacrifice. That's what it means when the passage says that "our spiritual sacrifices are made acceptable to God through Jesus."

But Jesus didn't stop serving us on the cross.

As long as there is a church, Jesus will serve the church as its cornerstone.

I used to look at the word *cornerstone* and think of rank and importance. The cornerstone is the largest and most important rock in the whole building.

But the cornerstone is actually great because of its *service*.

The cornerstone is at the bottom of the pile. It's buried underground, never to see the light of day. A cornerstone is covered with dirt and crawled across by worms and grubs. The cornerstone endures dampness and cold.

No one sees the cornerstone or notices the weight it bears. Its job is to make the building possible.

Jesus is our cornerstone. He holds up the weight of our strengths, weaknesses, half-baked ideas, addictions, sinful patterns, and quirks. He transforms us from a pile of bricks into an interconnected "house of worship."

And he does this through servanthood.

Going back to our theater metaphor—Jesus is the Executive Producer of our drama. Yet he serves us as a Stagehand.

"A student is not above his teacher, nor a servant above his master."
—Jesus in Matthew 10:24

You get the point.

Stagehands, God bless you. You are God's gift to every type of leader. Through your flexibility and selflessness, you show the rest of us how to lead like Jesus.

some action steps

Servanthood isn't natural, and while there are no Seven Steps to Instant Heart Change and Servanthood, there are spiritual disciplines worth pursuing if you want to develop the Stagehand style of leadership.

• Pray for your team.

Leadership isn't about you. Make a habit of lifting your team up in prayer. As you do so, you'll start seeing what they truly need from you.

And you'll become motivated to be the answer to your own prayers as you step up and serve them.

Make an appointment in your PDA to pray for your team.

Prayer worked for Ezra.

• Immerse yourself in Stagehand stories.

Servanthood is counterintuitive. It requires a complete rewiring of how we think—a renewing of our mind.

Comb through Scriptures and look for servanthood stories. Jesus' life is the perfect starting point. Read the accounts of servant leaders that I summarized earlier in the chapter. Marinate your mind in these stories until you value what these Stagehands valued—servanthood.

• Inform your style.

No one is asking you to stop being a Director, a Production Assistant, or a Drama Coach. By all means, if God hard-wired you to be a visionary, don't stop.

Yesterday I had lunch with a Christian leader who was struggling with this issue. He was being pressured by a director in his agency to exhibit servant leadership by doing front-line work. However, this leader knew that wasn't what he was hired to do.

> **Make an appointment in your PDA to pray for your team.**

His job was fund raising and creating a visible profile for his nonprofit organization. If he were to block off time to personally tutor the children of migrant workers, the agency would suffer over time when the cash stopped flowing into the agency.

So what was he to do?

By the end of lunch, he realized that for him, being a Stagehand meant that he'd spend more time developing his team leaders. He'd be their mentor and help build their profile in the community—even if that meant that they became more marketable and left the agency.

This leader decided that for his situation, servanthood meant seeking the best in his employees.

What does servanthood look like for you?

God is not calling you to abandon your post. Don't run out and violate your commitment to your job description by filling your days with random acts of servanthood.

Instead, transform your job description. Leverage your leadership with a Stagehand's heart.

Imagine the results.

Let's be truthful: We all need to see that our work brings results. If we get a sense that we aren't being effective or making a difference, we get discouraged. And when we get discouraged, we slow down—and maybe stop.

That tendency makes servanthood hazardous work, because much of the work of servanthood is done "backstage." No one sees the results of what you do—not even you. The seeds you're sowing often won't produce a harvest for a decade or more.

So *imagine* the results. It's OK.

The seeds you're sowing often won't produce a harvest for a decade or more.

Imagine what could happen with your team if the members became energized by your words of encouragement. How much more productive would they be?

How much more positive would your teachers be if you quietly cleaned their classrooms on occasion and thanked them for their faithful work? How would the positive attitude that resulted improve their willingness to connect with kids? How might that change kids' lives?

Get the idea?

Look, you can let your imagination run wild and become a legend in your own mind, giving pretend interviews to adoring reporters who are covering your induction into the Servanthood Hall of Fame.

Or you can use your imagination to have faith that, in Paul's words, "Your labor in the Lord is not in vain" (1 Corinthians 15:58).

Play the part.

Now it's time to do it. You might not feel like a servant. You might not be thinking like a servant. The self-centered parts of you might be internally grumbling.

That's all right. You aren't being a hypocrite by taking the first wobbly steps toward being a deeper servant. People don't call toddlers little hypocrites, do they? Nor a student airplane pilot for that matter.

It doesn't matter if you're learning to crawl or fly as a Stagehand—just start taking the next steps. Eventually, you'll behave yourself into a next level Stagehand.

So let's get cracking, shall we?

Make an action plan for your next steps. Responding to the following might help...

• Do you have a volunteer who's struggling in his or her personal life?

• Does your senior pastor need encouragement?

• Is there a mess that needs cleaned up in one of your classrooms?

• Could you help a single mom sign her children into three different classrooms at the same time on Sunday morning?

• How can you turbo-charge your leadership style through consistent acts of servanthood?

Do you have your own ideas? Write them down, and get them done.

not a means, but the end

In his book, *Uprising: A Revolution of the Soul,* Erwin McManus makes a powerful observation. All throughout Jesus' career, he seemed to be in a wrestling match with his disciples to convince them about the value of servanthood.

The disciples joined Jesus, God himself, on a three-year, nonstop service project. They participated in Jesus' preaching and healing ministry, and they even had the honor of being sent out to serve without Jesus' immediate supervision.

And somehow, throughout the entire time, they viewed servanthood as something they'd do for a season before being promoted into greatness.

The disciples served, but they bickered over who would get the highest rank in God's kingdom.

"When this serving stuff stops, who will be the greatest officer in the kingdom? Who gets the corner office with a window at the Kingdom of God Headquarters?"

In McManus' words:

"Everyone kept hoping that if they served long enough they would find a different outcome in the end. Servanthood is not God's way to get us to the place where we will only be served; it is both the way and the life of the kingdom of God."[3]

Jesus had to keep bringing them back to reality.

"The Son of Man did not come to be served, but to serve, and to give his life as a ransom for many."

"A student is not above his teacher, nor a servant above his master."

The disciples wanted to be servants as an *end* to eventually being served. Jesus wanted them to understand that the highest rung on the ladder of spiritual maturity *is* servanthood. It doesn't get any better than being a servant.

Servants get God. They behave like God behaves, so they have a window into God's motivation and heart. As hard as it is to believe and understand, God glorifies himself by being a servant. That's what God does. And God never changes.

Servanthood isn't the vegetables you endure to get to dessert. It *is* the dessert.

> **Servanthood isn't the vegetables you endure to get to dessert. It *is* the dessert.**

You might be a lot more spiritual than I am, but I struggle to believe and live that last sentence. Yet, the most beautiful thing that can ever happen to your soul and mine is that we join God in servanthood forever.

Servanthood isn't a means to a far off Easy Street, but is a gateway to helping us be a little more like God. And as we become more like God, we grow in our capacity to understand and enjoy him.

Again, if you are a Stagehand, please don't ever feel self-conscious about the way God wired you to lead. True, your style *does* tend to be overlooked. There's not a whole lot of glamour attached to it. But that's because, in Christ, we are all still relearning to appreciate the things of God.

Thanks for being an example.

a stagehand's prayer

Dear God,

    Your servant heart amazes me. You are the creator of the universe, yet you humble yourself and serve humanity every moment of the day. Thank you for making me your servant. God, help me to serve with flexibility, with cheerfulness, and with diligence.

    Protect my heart from serving out of pride and from judging people who don't serve the way I do.

    Make my work matter, God. May it help your kingdom come.

    In Jesus' name, amen.

for reflection and discussion

1. Does your children's ministry honor its Stagehands? How do you affirm the Stagehands on your team?

2. How would you rate your servanthood index on a scale of 1 to 10? What can you do to increase your willingness to serve others?

3. If you aren't a natural Stagehand, what would *your* leadership style look like if you turbo-charged it with Stagehand tendencies? What impact would this have on your children's ministry?

Endnotes

1. Yes, the word is literally *deaconess.* But the way I understand the Greek, that's an issue of how gender changes the ending of a word. It's similar to the English word for *steward* and *steward-ess*—gender is designated but they have the same function on an airplane. I haven't found Paul mentioning the qualifications of deaconess in the Pastoral Epistles, so I'll stick with the translation, *deacon.* Believe me, I'm not trying to make the definitive statement on the role of women in the church. People smarter than I am have been disagreeing on this for centuries. I'm not attempting to answer the question, "Did Phoebe help govern the church through the power of an official position?" I'm saying *she led the church.* Regardless of the theological disagreements that fill the church over this issue, I hope all will see Phoebe as an exceptional servant leader.
2. Check out Philippians 2:25-30 for an example.
3. McManus, Erwin Raphael, *Uprising: A Revolution of the Soul* (Nashville, TN: Thomas Nelson, Inc., 1993), 251.

CHAPTER 9

leadership style summaries

Use these handy handouts to share *what you've learned with your team.*

Whew! You've been working hard...and taking in a *lot* of information.

Let's make sure you can keep track of it—and communicate it to others.

The following summaries of each leadership style will help you share what you've learned with your team, your pastor, and with others who want to better understand the dynamics of your ministry.

Make as many copies as you need for your church's children's ministry. The more your teams adopt and use these terms and definitions, the more your team will value each member's unique leadership contribution. And the more individual team members will consider their leadership contributions important.

Director Leadership Style Summary

Description: Possesses the ability to visualize what "the play" will look like on Opening Night and is able to communicate that vision to an entire team. The Director uses that picture to motivate his or her team to action. In a ministry context, the Director is able to see what the children's ministry can accomplish for God if it steps boldly into the future.

Inspiration:

1. I constantly find myself dreaming about the unrealized potential of my ministry.

2. I study both Scripture and other thriving ministries to discover what direction I should lead my ministry.

Affirmation:

1. I feel satisfaction when I am able to mobilize my teams to tackle a big, formidable goal.

2. I enjoy being a pioneer and blazing a new path for my ministry.

Implementation:

1. I lead by telling others stories of what our ministry could look like.

2. I have an easy time asking people to make deep personal sacrifices for the sake of the ministry and achieving "the dream."

Frustration:

1. I often feel as if I'm waiting for others in my ministry to catch up or get "on board."

2. I am annoyed by people who have a hard time seeing the big picture.

Ministry Star(s):
The Promised Land, Muscle

Leadership Energy:
Vision

Production Assistant Leadership Style Summary

Description: In theater, this person works closely with the Director to help him or her move the team to the goal. The Production Assistant develops the master calendars—the rehearsal schedules, advertising schedules, and set design schedules. In a ministry context, the Production Assistant bridges the status quo to the Director's vision through a series of well-defined and logically progressing steps. A skillful Production Assistant is able to manage the change of attitudes and "buy-in" of teammates and influential people in the congregation.

Inspiration:

1. I quickly break large projects into a series of manageable steps.

2. I am able to quickly identify what resources, volunteers, and budgets need to be in place in order to lead my organization through change in an orderly fashion.

Affirmation:

1. I enjoy it when my team leader turns to me to develop the plan to make his or her vision become a reality.

2. I feel most valuable to the team when my skills are used to help the team move through change with efficiency and minimal levels of conflict.

Implementation:

1. I lead by developing calendars, timelines, and to-do lists that help our team measure its progress as we move toward our goals.

2. I lead by helping the team and congregation manage its emotional responses to a large task or change by giving them constructive opportunities to share their opinions and feelings.

Frustration:

1. I am frustrated by leaders who initiate change before taking the time to think through implications of that change.

2. I am frustrated by leaders who deviate from a plan on which the team has agreed.

Ministry Star:
Maps

Leadership Energy:
Strategy

Stage Manager Leadership Style Summary

Description: The Stage Manager has an eye for all the details that need to be attended to in order for the play to be successfully produced. In a ministry setting, the Stage Manager has an eye for the systems and to-do lists that need to be attended to for the ministry to run efficiently.

Inspiration:

1. I am able to mentally organize my ministry into a series of systems that need to be organized.

2. I constantly look for new ways to improve the efficiency of how things happen in my ministry.

Affirmation:

1. I take pleasure in creating an orderly environment in which people can serve.

2. I feel secure when I operate within clearly defined boundaries and expectations.

Implementation:

1. I lead by creating policies and systems to help others do their jobs well.

2. I have an eye for detail and am constantly generating to-do lists to organize my day.

Frustration:

1. I have difficulty understanding those who ignore details and protocol.

2. I dislike working in unstructured environments.

Ministry Star:
Muscle

Leadership Energy:
Organization

Drama Coach Leadership Style Summary

Description: In theater, the Drama Coach leads by teaching others the skills and competencies needed to become skilled actors. In a ministry context, the Drama Coach leads by teaching team members the competencies, values, policies and procedures, and philosophies needed for the team to become master children's ministry volunteers.

Inspiration:

1. I am able to teach skills and concepts to my team members so they have the best chance for being successful in ministry.

2. I can present both Scriptures and my children's ministry knowledge in simple and memorable ways that prompt people to change their behavior.

Affirmation:

1. I enjoy studying Scripture as well as a broad field of literature in the business and education fields so I can bring the best ideas into my ministry.

2. I feel most used by God when I am leading a classroom, whether it's filled with children or adults.

Implementation:

1. I constantly create opportunities to equip my team members in group or individual settings.

2. I have identified a curriculum of skills and theory that I believe my team members need to understand in order to be effective children's ministers.

Frustration:

1. I am frustrated when my team members do not take advantage of the teacher training opportunities available to them.

2. I often find myself analyzing teachers who I sit under and find myself developing better ways to present the same material.

Ministry Star:
Toolbox

Leadership Energy:
Equipping

Theater Manager Leadership Style Summary

Description: In the world of drama, the Theater Manager provides a healthy environment in which everyone can work. He or she pays the heating bills and makes sure that the rehearsal rooms and stage are clean. In a ministry environment, the Theater Manager creates a healthy relational and cognitive environment that promotes productive ministry.

Inspiration:

1. I am primarily motivated by the belief that healthy ministries flow from healthy teams and individuals.

2. I constantly gauge the emotional and attitudinal health of my team.

Affirmation:

1. I feel most satisfied when there is a positive sense of well-being among my team members.

2. I enjoy tending to the personalities of my teams and ministry.

Implementation:

1. I am able to lead my teams through powerful emotional experiences that shape my team's attitudes and morale.

2. I am able to unite a diverse group of people into a common culture using training, symbols, experiences, and music.

Frustration:

1. I become frustrated when I see team members exhibiting attitudes that harm our group's well-being.

2. I am frustrated by leaders who act without considering how their behavior will affect the team's morale.

Ministry Star(s):

Has a global influence on Promised Land, Maps, Toolbox, Heart, and Muscle.

Leadership Energy:

Health

Stagehand Leadership Style Summary

Description: In theater, the Stagehand advances the progress of the team by meeting the physical needs of the team. Stagehands build the set and make sure that all of the props are acquired and working. In a ministry setting, the Stagehand serves the team by meeting their physical needs and allowing other leaders to focus on their roles.

Inspiration:

1. I am able to anticipate what supplies and labor the team will need in order to accomplish its goals.

2. I'd rather be of assistance to the people who are doing the lead work.

Affirmation:

1. I enjoy working behind the scenes to support my more visible team members.

2. I take pride in my flexibility and willingness to do whatever it takes to get the job done.

Implementation:

1. I tend to volunteer for the set-up and tear-down phases of most events.

2. I lead by doing all the menial jobs that can pile up and get in the way of the team accomplishing its goals.

Frustration:

1. I can find myself feeling forgotten by the rest of the team.

2. I can be judgmental of team members who overlook the physical jobs that need to be done in the ministry.

Ministry Star:
Muscle

Leadership Energy:
Servanthood

^{my} **leadership profile worksheet**

Create a personalized self-profile of *your leadership style as you collect what you've learned in previous chapters, and prayerfully consider how God is using you in leadership.*

Sometimes it *is* all about you...and this is one of those times.

Use the following pages to create a personalized self-profile of your leadership style. You'll collect what you've learned in previous chapters and prayerfully consider how God is using you in leadership.

Note the word *prayerfully* in the previous sentence.

Don't slam through these pages in an effort to complete the profile as quickly as possible. God has been taking his time shaping you; it's worth your taking a bit of time as you appreciate what God has been up to.

You're unique. Valuable. Precious. Gifted.

Take all the time it takes to let those truths sink in.

A. My top two leadership styles are… (from page 33).

1._____

2._____

B. My leadership motivations are… (transfer the "Inspiration" statements from the two profiles you scored highest on).

1._____

2._____

3._____

4._____

C. My leadership methods are… (transfer the "Implementation" statements from the two profiles you scored highest on).

1._____

2._____

3._____

4._____

D. My leadership is most affirmed when… (transfer the two "Affirmation" statements from your top two profiles which *most* capture when you feel your leadership being affirmed).

1._____

2._____

E. I am most frustrated as a leader when… (transfer the two "Frustration" statements from your top two profiles which *most* capture when you feel your leadership being frustrated).

1._____

2._____

F. I contribute to the following children's ministry stars... (please list the ministry stars associated with your top two styles).

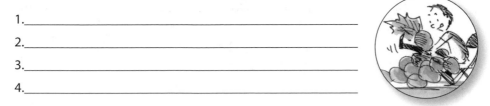

1._____
2._____
3._____
4._____

G. The type of energy I contribute to the team is... (please list "Leadership Energy" statements from your top two styles).

1._____
2._____

H. My leadership blind spots are... (Review your results from the Dramatic Leadership Test on page 33. Note your two lowest scores. Now turn to the Style Summaries on pages 168-173. Write down the "Leadership Energy" words from your profiles with the lowest scores.)

1._____
2._____
3._____
4._____

I. Are you able to fully use your leadership style in children's ministry? Why or why not?

_____
_____
_____
_____
_____
_____

J. Describe your dream job in children's ministry. What role in your children's ministry would allow you to best lead the way God made you?

_____

_____

_____

_____

_____

_____

K. What are the barriers that keep you from operating out of your primary leadership style? How can you remove those barriers? Who on your team can help you?

_____

_____

_____

_____

_____

_____

L. This is my personal leadership growth agenda…. (In each chapter, you were invited to identify leadership skills that you wished to build into your style. Flip through the chapters and write your agenda here.)

_____

_____

_____

_____

_____

_____

This is who I will tell about my growth agenda:

_____

This is my action plan: *(Make your plan measurable and concrete, and include deadlines.)*

What I'll do	How I'll do it	When I'll start and finish

M. This is how I will transform my leadership style by infusing ever-increasing servanthood...

_____

_____

_____

_____

CHAPTER (11)

assembling
your cast

You've been on a remarkable journey of self-discovery. Chances are that if you didn't know already, you now know how you're wired as a leader. You have a handle on your style, your strengths, and your weaknesses. So you're ready to roll, right?

Not so fast, Speedy.

You'd be set if you were the only leader in your children's ministry or church. But you are decidedly *not* the only show in town. That's not how Jesus builds a ministry. We visited this passage at the beginning of the book, but it's time to revisit it.

"It was he who gave some to be apostles, some to be prophets, some to be evangelists, and some to be pastors and teachers, to prepare God's people for works of service, so that the body of Christ may be built up until we all reach unity…

"From him the whole body, joined and held together by every

supporting ligament, grows and builds itself up in love, as each part does it's work" (Ephesians 4:11-13a, 16).

If these six chapters on leadership styles haven't convinced you that God doesn't honor one "silver bullet" style of leadership, I hope this passage does. Consider the different spiritual gifts that God places under the hood of the leaders of the church. That's quite a diverse array of spiritual gifts in church leadership.

And each one of those gifts produces a different leadership voice in the person who was given the gift!

The good people that God has surrounded you with weren't placed there to be extensions of you.

God didn't intend these leaders to go off into their own corner of the church and do their own thing. Verse 16 paints a picture of the unity that a diverse team of leaders can enjoy. Some leaders provide muscle. Some provide bone. Some supply the ligaments and tendons. All weave themselves together and grow in love until only one thing is visible—Jesus.

I can't accomplish that type of beauty all by myself. In all my years of serving, I will never be able to transform my children's department into the Body of Christ—not by myself. Neither can you.

We desperately need to operate in teams if we ever want the product of our energy to be Jesus.

There's no other way.

It's not enough for you to know your style, and it's not enough for your co-workers to know your style. The good people that God has surrounded you with weren't placed there to be extensions of you. And for that they are *thankful*.

You might very well be the point person. The buck might stop with you. You might feel all alone in bearing the torch for your children's ministry. But you aren't the only leader in your ministry.

How do I know this?

The Bible tells me so.

God gives leadership to churches and ministries in sets of two or more. Do you remember when Elijah had his emotional meltdown on Mount Horeb and told God that he was the only one doing the Lord's work?

Elijah was in a deep funk. I'm guessing that was, in part, because he had largely been leading like a lone ranger. Somehow, he'd forgotten his conversation with Obadiah—just paragraphs before. When the king ordered the execution of God's prophets, Obadiah hid 100 prophets in the caves.

Let's do some math. One hundred prophets, plus Obadiah. That's 101 leaders with whom Elijah could do ministry. And *still* Elijah saw himself as alone. When God ended Elijah's retreat at Camp Prozac, he instructed Elijah to create a mentoring team with Elisha.

God is not so cruel to make you do ministry alone.

So here's what you need to do: Gather up a team of your proven leaders and some potential leaders.

Start dreaming about what your children's ministry can be if you become a team.

If everyone on your team discovers his or her unique leadership style.

If everyone on your team becomes vulnerable and shares who they are—what they can add to the team and what weaknesses they need to have protected.

If in addition to sharing your styles with each other, you began to share *yourselves* with each other.

Once *that* happens, your team can have an Ephesians 4:16 moment. You can grow together and build yourselves up in love—until your ministry begins to look like Jesus.

I'm not going to lie to you. Building a team that healthy and that interconnected takes work. It's not instant. We're talking about a lifelong process that begins with communication—and lots of it.

Start dreaming about what your children's ministry can be if you become a team.

That's why I'm *not* going to supply you with pages of fancy charts that tell you how to make someone with the Director style dovetail with someone who has a Production Assistant style.

It's not that there aren't generalizations to be made. But you and your team aren't generalizations. You're all unique individuals. So instead of giving you charts that you could read in the privacy of your home, in the next few pages I'll give you a script—two scripts, actually.

They're for team experiences, two opportunities for your team to begin the journey of discovering how you can all lead the way God made you...together.

team experience one: DISCOVERING YOUR ROLE

Supplies
- Bibles
- copies of the American Film Institute's "100 Best Films" list (visit www.afi.com and download the information)—one per participant
- copies of the "Dramatic Leadership Assessment Test" (pp. 28-33)—one per participant
- copies of "My Leadership Profile Worksheet" (pp. 176-179)—one per participant
- red blanket or tablecloth
- five tennis balls
- bowl filled with grapes
- pencils
- one jar of honey
- one road map
- one toolbox
- large heart cut from red construction paper
- small dumbbell
- snacks—good stuff, too!

Getting Ready
Before the meeting, decorate the room with large stars cut from poster board, a director's chair, and a large pair of sunglasses cut from black poster board. Cut out lenses for the sunglasses from aluminum foil and tape them to the glasses. Set out snacks and beverages for the group to enjoy throughout the evening.

Line up a volunteer to play the part of Super Leader. Be sure to select a volunteer who can't juggle!

Objectives: Participants will discover the need for team-based leadership in your children's ministry and begin to identify their own leadership styles.

Introduction

Say **I'm glad you're all here! We're now beginning an important journey together—we're going to discover the secrets of running a five-star children's ministry! But speaking of five-star productions, I want to show you the American Film Institute's list of the top 100 films of all time.**

Pass out copies of the list, and ask participants to quickly scan the list. Then ask participants to form pairs and to discuss the following questions:

• **Are you surprised by any of the films that made the list or by their rank on the list? Why?**

• **What's your favorite film on the list? Why?**

• **Think about your favorite film. What made it great to you? What does it take for a film to be considered a five-star production?**

After participants have had the opportunity to discuss the questions, ask volunteers to share what they discussed.

Say **Let's think about our children's ministry as if it were a film or theater production. With your partner discuss:**

> We want to be a part of a ministry that helps children develop a vibrant friendship with Jesus.

• **What genre of film would you say our children's ministry is? Why?**

• **If our ministry were ranked by a film critic, would we be a one-star production, a five-star production, or somewhere in between? What ranking would we receive—and why?**

Five Stars and the Super Leader

Say: **We all want to be a part of excellent, five-star productions—including a five-star children's ministry that takes care of kids with kindness and safety. We want to be a part of a ministry that helps children develop a vibrant friendship with Jesus.**

But how do five-star ministries happen? Partly, it's leadership. We tend to turn to a single person for leadership—a charismatic, energetic person who loves kids and who we think can get the job done. We want a Super Leader!

There's no Super Leader who can cover all those bases.

Choose a volunteer to play the part of Super Leader. Have that person drape the blanket on his or her shoulders as a cape.

Say: **Super Leader, I'll list the five essential Stars of Effective Children's Ministry. As I mention each one, I'll hand you a tennis ball. Your job is to keep all five balls in the air. Ready?**

Mention the following five issues, handing a ball to your Super Leader as you do so:
- a Promised Land
- a Map
- a Toolbox
- Heart
- Muscle

Your volunteer will be unable to keep all the balls in the air at one time. Act surprised and disappointed. Ask the volunteer to surrender the Super Leader cape and have a seat. Lead your team in applauding the volunteer for a great effort.

Say: **Let me be clear: I couldn't have done even *that* well in keeping all these balls in the air at the same time! And when you hear all the leadership functions that have to be present in our ministry, you'll see why nobody could cover them all—there's no Super Leader who can cover all those bases.**

Hold up the bowl of grapes and honey.

Say: **The first star that every children's ministry needs is a Promised Land concept.**

Just as Moses motivated the Israelites by painting a picture of a land flowing with milk and honey, our children's ministry needs to have a picture of a "sweet place."

Our Promised Land is a picture of what our children's ministry would look like if were everything it could be. We need a leader to keep that dream in front of us in order to inspire us and give us

energy. Think of this as the vision of our ministry.

Hold up the road map.

Say: The second children's ministry star is a Map.

We know where our ministry is today. We know what our Promised Land is—what our ministry would be if it was everything it could be.

But how do we get there? We need a strategy or a road map to tell us how to move our children's ministry in the right direction.

Hold up the toolbox.

Say: The third ministry star is a Toolbox. Our ministry Toolbox is filled with all of the know-how needed to get ministry jobs done.

One tool might be knowing how to discipline kids in a classroom (that tool isn't the hammer, by the way!). Another tool might be a policy on getting reimbursed for an expense. A healthy children's ministry has a Toolbox stocked with the right tools to get any job done right!

Hold up the paper heart.

Say: The fourth children's ministry star is Heart.

By Heart, I mean a caring, high morale that's shared by everyone on the team. We all need to feel joy, courage, acceptance, challenge, and love. We need to have healthy relationships that are free from unresolved conflict and gossip.

Hold up the dumbbell.

Say: The final star is Muscle.

A children's ministry Muscle is exactly what it sounds like—hard work. It's the ability to meet deadlines and do whatever needs to be done to make a children's ministry fly.

Sometimes we think that just the visionary—the person talking about the Promised Land—is a real leader. That's not true. A healthy, growing ministry needs leadership in all the areas I've mentioned. In addition to a Promised Land vision, we also need the Map. We need tools in the Toolbox. We need a Heart that beats with God's love for children. And we need the Muscle to get things done.

> **Our ministry Toolbox is filled with all of the know-how needed to get ministry jobs done.**

Form trios and discuss the following questions:

• **How is trying to juggle too many balls like or unlike your life? your ministry here at church?**

• **Which ministry stars do we do a good job of keeping in the air? Why?**

• **Which ministry stars do we tend to drop? Why?**

• **How guilty is our ministry of turning to a Super Leader to bear the burden of supporting all five stars?**

• **Do you ever feel pressure to *be* the Super Leader? Why is that?**

Ask for volunteers to share the insights that emerged during the discussion.

Say: **Most children's ministries are tempted to look for Super Leaders who can handle all five stars. But having one person take care of all five stars doesn't work.**

Fortunately, there's a better way.

Have everyone move their chairs into a circle. Start tossing the balls into the circle and instruct everyone to work together to keep the "stars" in the air.

As team members throw the balls, ask them to discuss the following questions:

• **How well do we share the burden of supporting the five ministry stars as a team?**

• **Which star or stars are the easiest for you personally to support? Why?**

> **God didn't intend for any one person to create a five-star ministry all by himself or herself.**

Collect the tennis balls.

Read Ephesians 4:11-16.

Say: **God didn't intend for any one person to create a five-star ministry all by himself or herself. These verses tell us that God gives many different spiritual gifts that create different styles of leadership.**

God is kind. He doesn't expect any one person to bear the weight of leadership alone. God wired each one of us differently. He's given each of us a unique style that allows us to support *some* of the children's ministry stars. Let's take a few minutes to discover our styles.

Give each participant a copy of the Dramatic Leadership Assessment

Test and a pencil. Review the instructions on page 28. Give everyone 15 minutes to complete the assessment.

Draw participants' attention back to you. Use the Leader Style Summary Pages (Chapter 9) to help you quickly explain each leadership style. After you explain each style, ask participants if anyone fits this leadership description.

Say: **God has wired each of us differently—each of us has an ability to support at least one of the five different stars. Often we support more than one. Together, we can build a five-star ministry.**

Pass out copies of "My Leadership Profile Worksheet." Ask everyone to complete them before the next time you meet.

Say: **Let's close in prayer.**

Pray: **God, we love you. We want to honor you with a five-star ministry that helps children fall in love with you. God, thank you for giving us a team. The job is too big for anyone of us to do alone. Teach us how to work together to become a strong team. Amen.**

team experience two:
BECOMING AN ALL-STAR CAST

Supplies
- TV with VCR or DVD player
- copy of *Miracle* (Disney 2004)
- copies of the Dramatic Leadership Assessment Test (pp. 28-33)—one per participant
- pencils
- self-stick name tags
- markers
- roll of yellow crepe paper streamers
- snacks—good stuff, too!

Getting Ready
Before the meeting, contact participants and remind them to bring their completed "My Leadership Profile Worksheets." Use the same

decorations and props you used during the last session. Again, make snacks and beverages available to help create a warm and inviting environment.

As participants arrive, ask them to write their names on name tags and to leave space to write additional information on the tags.

Participants will begin to discover how *their* team can work together.

Objective: Participants will begin to discover how *their* team can work together to support the five stars of children's ministry.

Introduction: Miracle on Your Street!

Say: **Welcome back! During our last session, you began to discover how to lead the way God made you. In this session, we'll discover how we can lead the way God made us…together!**

By now, you have a rough idea about what your leadership style is. You've completed the "My Leadership Profile Worksheet," so you've had the chance to build a customized profile that fits you like a glove.

Ask if anyone has questions about the six styles or the five stars.

(**Facilitators:** If you are the only person who has read this book, it's going to be incumbent upon you to be fluent in the six styles. It's a good idea to read Chapters 3-8 again and to have a copy of "Leadership Style Summaries" [pp. 168-173] nearby.)

Say: **I want to show you a video clip from the movie *Miracle*. It's the story of the 1980 U.S. Olympic Hockey Team. For years, the U.S. team had been the doormat of the tournament, especially for the Soviets. In this scene, we'll see university coach Herb Brooks being interviewed by the Olympic Committee for the job.**

Use the DVD screen to select scene 1: "An Honorable Goal." If you are using a VCR, look for the scene to begin at about 3 minutes, 19 seconds into the movie.

Ask participants to respond to these questions:

• **Why was Coach Brooks so opposed to using all-star teams in the Olympics?**

• **How can relying too much on individual talent hurt our team?**

Say: **Coach Brooks *did* get the job and didn't waste any time installing his team-based approach to hockey. Let's take a peek at how Brooks went about selecting his players at tryouts.**

Show scene 2: "Making the Cut." If you are using a VCR, look for the scene to begin about 12 minutes, 12 seconds into the movie when Coach Brooks says, "Look at this."

After the clip, ask participants to form pairs and discuss these questions:

- **What did the coach mean when he said, "I'm not looking for the best players; I'm looking for the right players"?**
- **What would a "right player" look like on our team? Why?**

Say: **Having a winning team is a lot like that U.S. Hockey Team. We don't need to have one super star do it all. What we *do* need is for everyone in this room to feel comfortable leading out of their strengths, as well as knowing how to rely on the other people on the team to do what you can't do.**

I don't know about you, but that takes a lot of pressure off me.

For the remainder of our time together, we'll talk about our styles and how we can do a better job of working together. Feel free to refer to your worksheets during the discussion.

> ## tip
>
> Switching between the scenes requires concentration. Recruit a helper, and be sure your helper knows what scenes you're looking for—and how to recognize them—before your training session.

Ask participants to use markers to write their top one or two leadership styles on their name tags. This will help everyone remember everyone else's style and will make the conversation go more smoothly.

If you have 10 or fewer participants, sit in a circle so participants can see one another. If you have more than 10 participants, consider creating two (or more) circles.

Lead your team through the following discussion guide...

Go around the circle and ask each person to answer the following questions:

- **What do you bring to the table as a leader?**

- **What parts of your style are you most excited about? What do you like about the way you lead?**

Use this activity as an opportunity to affirm your leaders!

Continue through the following questions. Please note that as facilitator, you need to keep the conversation balanced and moving forward.

- **Are you able to fully use your leadership style to make our children's ministry a five-star enterprise? Why or why not? What changes would need to be made to allow you to fully use your gifts?**
- **In what ways do you feel your leadership style is valued by the team? In what ways could it be valued more fully?**
- **Which of the five children's ministry stars are you simply not wired for? Are you currently being expected to provide leadership in an area that you're not equipped to provide? Who in the room might be able to help you?**
- **Do you see any conflicts waiting to happen because of the gift diversity (or lack of diversity) on our team? Explain.**
- **How can we work to see our differences as strengths and not weaknesses?**

> In what ways do you feel your leadership style is valued by the team?

After you wrap up the discussion, show participants the props you've brought from your last session and explain the connection between the props and the five leadership stars:

- **Bowl of grapes and honey:** Providing a "Promised Land" vision
- **Road map:** Providing strategy and direction for reaching the Promised Land
- **Toolbox:** Providing training and skills
- **Paper heart:** Providing morale and encouraging healthy relationships
- **Dumbbell:** Providing muscle to get things done

Place the props on a table, and ask participants to stand around the table near the prop that represents the ministry star each person feels most equipped to provide. Ask:

- **Which stars seem to have the most people already providing** leadership? What are examples of how our ministry has thrived in these areas?

• Which stars aren't as well-supported? How have we seen the impact of these "falling stars"?

• What would our ministry look like if we could provide manpower and support for every area?

Ask participants to return to their circle(s). Ask:

• Do we need to make any changes to allow all of our current team members to lead from their strengths?

• What types of leaders should we add to our team to increase our effectiveness and impact?

Ask participants to brainstorm a list of people whom they believe have the abilities to bolster leadership areas that are currently weak on your team.

Keep this list for reference as you do targeted, specific recruiting in the future.

Closing Affirmation: Star Power

Have the group form a circle, facing in.

Hold onto one end of a yellow streamer roll, and toss it to one member of the group. Make a specific affirmation to that person, thanking them for a concrete way that they provide leadership for the whole team. Have that person hold the streamer with one hand, toss the streamer roll to a second team member, and then affirm that person's leadership. Repeat this until everyone has been affirmed and a crepe paper star has been formed. Instruct the group to continue holding the star while you pray.

Pray: **Dear God, we thank you for our team. You've placed every member of our team here on purpose. Thank you for that.**

Lord, when we work together, we shine like stars. Help us grow in unity and love so we can show your love to the children in the community. Amen.

epilogue

The six tired teammates looked like *they'd been gently tossed onto the overstuffed furniture. Worn but satisfied, they watched the video of the children's musical, interrupting to make comments and tease each other.*

After the curtain call, Debbie stopped the tape and turned to face her team.

"It's been quite a ride, hasn't it? I have some awards I'd like to give you."

Debbie reached into her bag. "Patricia, I'd like to give you this desk calendar."

Patricia looked at the calendar with a puzzled look. "Debbie, your name is written on the top of the calendar. I don't get it."

"You did such a good job keeping the musical on schedule that I've decided to delegate the management of my entire life to you. You're an amazing production assistant. You'll notice I wrote my name in pencil just in case you're not up for the task."

Debbie rummaged into the bag as the room chuckled. Debbie fished out a small desktop organizer.

"Susie, this is for your relentless pursuit of order. May your pencils always point in the same direction! You did a brilliant job of taking care of the details. Our ducks were in order—first by height and then alphabetically. You brought order and efficiency to everything you touched. You were a brilliant stage manager!"

Susie mock curtsied to the applause of everyone.

"Dan, I present you with this whistle. You were a great coach. You taught the children well. You made legitimate actors out of them."

Dan dangled the whistle from its string. "This brings back bad memories of gym class," he frowned with mock alarm. Dan held the whistle to his lips and threatened to blow it.

More laughter.

Next, Tom unwrapped a heart-shaped box of chocolates.

"Tom, you guarded our collective heart. You made sure the adults and the children were building godly relationships as we did God's work. You even got the Joneses to host the cast party for the children. That went a long way toward repairing the tensions of the past week. Great work."

"And finally, Steve."

Debbie reached into her bag once again.

"Steve, you made my day. I thought I was going to be up half of last night setting up for the musical. Your servanthood allowed me to get the sleep I needed so I could lead well on Opening Night. And I actually got to enjoy the show."

Steve unwrapped his gift and held up a worship CD.

"This is to help you continue to serve cheerfully. Thanks for the way you lead! Now everyone, let's go eat."

Patricia interrupted. "Not so fast, Debbie. We have a gift for you."

A momentary wave of embarrassment and surprise flashed over Debbie's face as Dan quickly ducked out of the room and returned with a large box. Debbie composed herself and then carefully unwrapped the box. Inside she discovered a director's chair and a T-shirt with the musical logo on the front and the word "Director" screened across the back.

Patricia spoke, and it was obvious she was speaking for everyone.

"Debbie, this musical wouldn't have happened without you. You created the energy that got the ball rolling. That ball became an avalanche that forced us all to discover our leadership styles so we could stay on top of things. Thanks."

Debbie quickly wiped away the tears that were beginning to stream down her face.

"Gang. I asked God for a musical. He gave me a team. Thank you. Thank you all."

Debbie's team stayed together and produced several more musicals over the years. I'd be lying if I said that every moment of their existence was as magical as that scene at their victory party. Conflicts brewed from time to time. Debbie continued to launch new initiatives without tapping her production assistant for strategy tips. Dan's job forced him to relocate. The infamous Mrs. Jones took her place on the team, which caused new chemistry issues among the team members.

Over time, a community of proven leaders emerged.

Still, with every new challenge there was a new milestone to celebrate. Over time, a community of proven leaders emerged.

As I write, Lance Armstrong has just won his sixth straight Tour de France. I'm not up on cycling, but one of my SportsCenter-savvy co-workers brought me up to speed on an interesting fact: There are nine members on the U.S. Postal Service Cycling Team.

Can you name them?

How about two of them?

I didn't think so. But everyone knows Lance.

During the ESPN interview, a reporter asked one of the anonymous eight what his role was on the team. His reply? "I do whatever it takes to ensure the success of Lance Armstrong."

Imagine that. Eight people training their bodies year round to make someone else look good. The early mornings, the weight lifting, the hours logged on the bikes, the strict diets, learning to work with each other; all of these sacrifices for the glory of someone else. All for Lance Armstrong.

Now imagine this: *You* can belong to a team of leaders that's every bit as dedicated as Lance Armstrong's team. You can train together and discover how to each make your own unique contribution to the team. You can be up early, sleep late, and reorient your entire lives around the success of another—Jesus Christ.

> **"I press on toward the goal to win the prize for which God has called me heavenward in Christ Jesus."**

In case you missed it, that's the point of everything you've read in this book.

I didn't write this book to become rich or a children's ministry celebrity. In a handful of years, you'll be able to buy this book for a nickel at a garage sale.

I hope you didn't read this book to find the secrets to making your ministry problems disappear. When you solve the challenges of a one-star children's ministry, you have to face the challenges of a two-star children's ministry. Four-star children's ministries have their own headaches. It's part of the game.

My prayer is that this book will help you and me become like Lance Armstrong's team—unsung riders.

Use this book to discover how God wired you for leadership.

Use this book as a template to discover how you can broaden your leadership repertoire.

Use this book as a springboard for discussion with your teams to become more united toward a common purpose—the victory and fame of Jesus.

"I press on toward the goal to win the prize for which God has called me heavenward in Christ Jesus" (Philippians 3:14).

What is our prize?

My partners in ministry, this is our trophy: the victory and fame of Jesus. Our greatest gain is to ride with Jesus and to someday touch his trophy.

God bless you on this journey.

EVALUATION FOR
Lead the Way God Made You

Please help Group Publishing, Inc., continue to provide innovative and useful resources for ministry. Please take a moment to fill out this evaluation and mail or fax it to us. Thanks!

Group Publishing, Inc.
Attention: Product Development
P.O. Box 481
Loveland, CO 80539
Fax: (970) 292-4370

● ● ●

1. As a whole, this book has been (circle one)

not very helpful   *very helpful*

1   2   3   4   5   6   7   8   9   10

2. The best things about this book:

3. Ways this book could be improved:

4. Things I will change because of this book:

5. Other books I'd like to see Group publish in the future:

6. Would you be interested in field-testing future Group products and giving us your feedback? If so, please fill in the information below:

Name _____

Church Name _____

Denomination _____ Church Size _____

Church Address _____

City _____ State _____ ZIP _____

Church Phone _____

E-mail _____